FLY FISHING MADE EASY

Praise for a previous edition

"A worthwhile start for the novice fly fisherman."
—*Sports Afield*

"Rutter and Card give complete fly fishing instructions for beginners, hints for experts, and funny fish tales for everybody."
—*News-Journal* (Longview, Tex.)

"Everything you need to know about getting ahead in fly fishing."
—*Tribune & Times* (Tampa)

"The manual covers all the basics for the beginner, complete with clearly written and easy-to-use illustrations, but it also has enough meat for the most experienced angler."
—*Atlanta Journal-Constitution*

"A perfect 'how-to' guide for the fledgling fly caster as well as an excellent reference manual for any expert's library."
—*Small Press*

Help Us Keep This Guide Up-to-Date

Every effort has been made by the authors and editors to make this guide as accurate and useful as possible. However, many things can change after a guide is published—establishments close, phone numbers change, facilities come under new management, etc.

We would love to hear from you concerning your experiences with this guide and how you feel it could be made better and be kept up-to-date. While we may not be able to respond to all comments and suggestions, we'll take them to heart, and we'll also make certain to share them with the authors. Please send your comments and suggestions to the following address:

The Globe Pequot Press
Reader Response/Editorial Department
P.O. Box 480
Guilford, CT 06437

Or you may e-mail us at:

editorial@globe-pequot.com

Thanks for your input, and happy fishing!

MADE EASY SERIES

FLY FISHING MADE EASY

*A Manual for Beginners
with Tips for the Experienced*

Fourth Edition

Michael Rutter

and

Dave Card

FALCON GUIDE®

GUILFORD, CONNECTICUT
HELENA, MONTANA

AN IMPRINT OF THE GLOBE PEQUOT PRESS

FALCONGUIDE ®

All photos by Michael Rutter and David Carr

Library of Congress Cataloging-in-Publication Data

Rutter, Michael, 1953-
    Fly fishing made easy : a manual for beginners with
tips for the experienced / Michael Rutter and Dave
Card. — 4th ed.
        p. cm. — (Made easy series) (A Falcon guide)
    Includes index.
    ISBN-13: 978-0-7627-4118-2
    ISBN-10: 0-7627-4118-X
    1. Fly fishing. I. Card, Dave. II. Title.
SH456.R87 2007
799.12'4—dc22
                                                                    2006048530

Manufactured in the United States of America
Fourth Edition/First Printing

To buy books in quantity for corporate use
or incentives, call **(800) 962–0973, ext. 4551,**
or e-mail **premiums@GlobePequot.com.**

We would like to acknowledge our wives,
Shari and Lisa, for their help and support.

We would like to recognize our fishing buddies,
even if they do tell whoppers, for their friendship.

Contents

Preface

If you read this book, you will learn fly fishing.

You must know, however, that fly casting becomes a way of life, and there's nothing you can do to change it. You'll be constantly evolving as the face of fly casting itself is continually changing, beckoning you to higher levels.

It doesn't matter if you fish a hundred days a year or if you only unpack your fly rod for an occasional weekend outing. Every time you step into the water, fly rod in hand, you'll experience something new and something the same. There is no gender barrier, no racial barrier, no social barrier. It's just you, water, and fish.

You'll start to look at the world as a fly caster. When someone asks what you do, unless you catch yourself first, you'll say, "I fish with flies."

If you're like most of us, you'll get infected by the *fever* somewhere between the time you pick up a rod and the time you hook a fish. Casting gives you a reason to be double minded—and equally important, a reason to endure so you can get back to the water as soon as possible. You'll notice that when you aren't thinking at all, or when you're supposed to be thinking about "important" things, your mind will play games with you. It's part of the fever. Your fancy will take you to a calm alpine lake with a surface like glass and large trout indiscriminately taking flies off the film. You'll think of gin-clear streams with wooded sides and sweet mountain air and a stone fly hatch even the biggest rainbow can't resist.

You'll see a large brown trout taking a #18 Adams and rushing for the edge of the beaver pond. You'll feel the solid pressure as you gently lift the rod tip, setting the hook. You'll feel the quiver as a square-tailed brown pumps your rod and strains the light tippet. Then, the final Homeric run, the whirring line; you're stripped into the backing. You work the trout, gain a little, lose a little. After a five-minute eternity, the fish is closer. At last you gently slide your net into

No matter how long you've been fishing, you'll always feel a quiver when a fine fish takes your fly and you do battle.

Catching a fish with flies goes beyond the grin on your face.... It's a lifestyle.

the water. You admire the chocolate-colored belly and bright spots as you ease out the hook and return the trophy to the stream. You eagerly take in deep lungfuls of pine-scented breath and know most assuredly that you are alive.

Someone bumps you abruptly and shouts something obscene. Your reverie is gone, the lunker brown is gone. You realize a little sadly that the rod was actually your briefcase handle, the pine-scented breeze was automobile and diesel exhaust, and you are holding up an anxious line of commuters for the subway. Still, the silly grin plastered across your face defies the rush-hour hubbub. You'd rather be fishing, but you're feeling good anyway—because you know that sometime in the future you'll be fly fishing, and that makes it all worthwhile. You've learned that throwing flies is a vocation, a point of view, a philosophy—and for some, a religion. At the least, it's a way of life.

1

AN INTRODUCTION TO THE GREATEST SPORT ON EARTH

Why Fly Fish?

Why fly fish?

There is a certain romance associated with fly fishing. Casting a fly with a heavy line boasts a wonderful tradition—almost a mystique—one can't ignore. It's a style of angling that is precise, perhaps even poetic. It's the only kind of fishing that's thrilling even when the fish aren't cooperating.

Okay, you may say. It looks like a blast, and there's a 400-year tradition. But fly fishing seems so hard. What about all those different lines and leaders, wet flies and dry flies, mending, knots—let alone casting? Looks pretty confusing.

Where would you start? Are you sure anyone can learn?

Fly fishing may seem mystical at first, but there's nothing magical about it. Throwing a fly is a wonderful sport with a rich legacy, but *it's a learned skill*. And like learning any new skill (golf, tennis, skeet shooting, waterskiing), the process seems more complex than it really is. If you look at fly fishing as a series of simple steps, it's not complicated at all. In fact, if you can cast a spinning rod, you can fly fish. Fly-casting skills are not something you are born with—they are learned. This book will show you how.

Why fly fish? Here's eleven pounds of good reason. Our fishing buddy, Ken, is holding a nice rainbow he hooked on a #16 Prince Nymph. Casting wet flies is a great way to spend a late-fall afternoon. This fish took nearly a half hour to land.

You're never too young to start. Abbey Rutter started fly casting with her father when she was a toddler. Now she's in junior high and can cast a fly with the best of them.

Casting is the backbone of fly fishing. It's not hard—it just takes practice. When you finish reading this book, you will know how to cast.

The hardest part about learning a new skill, like fly fishing, is figuring out where to start, which is far more complicated than learning how to cast. Purchasing this book was a wise choice, because it will take some of the guesswork out of where to start and what to do. We've outlined the basic skills you need to know in clear, easy-to-follow chapters. Fly fishing isn't as difficult as many would have you believe. Sure, it takes a while to master all the elements, but with a little practice, you can be on the water hooking a fish.

Fly fishing is, gratefully, a lifetime sport you'll never outgrow. That doesn't mean, however, you have to wait years to catch fish! Or even weeks, for that matter. How about right away! The nice thing is you can grow at your own rate. After learning a few simple steps, you are ready. And before long, you'll be catching more fish than you caught with your spinning rod.

In the following chapters, you will master the basic elements of fly fishing. Specifically, you will learn:

• How to select a fly rod and reel
• How to choose a fly line
• How to fly fish
• How to present your fly
• How to judge the water
• How to select flies

We will look at the differences between wet and dry flies and how to fish each. We'll look at a variety of fishing strategies so that if one approach isn't working, you can use another. We might even slip in a fishing tale or two about the one that got away— and a few that didn't. And since we're getting acquainted, we'll consider a few of our embarrassing moments—like the time Michael's brand-new float tube was punctured by a mad bluegill in the middle of a lake (it's not often a half-pound sunfish can make a 200-pound man cry for help). Or the time Dave's waders were frozen solid to a large, red rock on the Green River (he unwisely sat down for a rest while wearing the wet waders on a January fishing trip and couldn't get up; he finally slid out of the waders and pried them loose).

As we've said, some will have you believe fly fishing is *very* difficult. We know otherwise, because we've taught hundreds of people how to cast. We'll look at everything you need to know. We think you'll find that learning how to cast and catch fish with a fly is delightful.

Jon-Michael Rutter caught a 23-inch cutthroat on his first fly fishing trip. He's now in college and still finds time to fish with his father.

2

THE RIGHT STUFF

Essential Fly Fishing Equipment

It's important to get the right stuff.

No question about it, fly casting is a gear-oriented sport. If it seems to you like a maze at first, you're not alone. Starting off with the right equipment will give you an edge. And while you won't have to take a second mortgage on your house, getting set up will cost more than it takes to go spin casting. In this chapter we'll introduce the equipment a beginning fly caster realistically needs to effectively catch fish with flies (not what a store clerk on commission might recommend).

We'll look at some of the items you can't do without. Then we'll talk about equipment you might want to add later but don't actually need at the moment. We'll also discuss a few odds and ends you might find beneficial—tools that help make the sport more enjoyable but can be acquired as your budget allows. Like furnishing a house or apartment, few of us can get it all at once.

We will present a general overview on each of the essential topics and help you answer a few pointed questions: What will your budget allow you to spend? How much do you dare spend? What type of fishing will you do? What sort of water do you expect to be on? How often do you plan to fish?

With so many equipment choices to make, it's hard to know where to start. We'll help you sort it out.

Although fly fishing is a skill-related sport, the equipment you fish with is important.

Casting is gear-oriented. There are certain things you can't do without, such as a good rod.

Need help? Match the rod to the type of fish you plan to catch.

Let's Start with the Rod

It boils down to one thing: When you're fishing, it's you and the rod.

You bond with your fishing rod. It allows you to cast your line a dozen different ways. It acts as a telegraph when you have a strike. It functions as a shock absorber when you work a fish. It lets you know when you're straining the tippet, the tapered mono line that attaches to your hook. The crisp action of the rod lets you mend, adjust your line on the water. It's a source of pride. It's a friend. Give it a name if you must.

The fly rod will be your biggest investment. Along with your fly line, it's the most critical factor in determining how well you cast and how much you enjoy the sport of fly fishing. Selecting a rod is one of the most difficult decisions you'll make. Rods come in a great range of prices, lengths, weights, and fishing orientations. Buying a rod is something you don't want to rush into. Take your time. If you have a friend who has a spare, see if you can borrow it while you learn to cast—maybe even for a few fishing trips. There are a lot of factors to consider. The more you know about this sport, the easier it is to buy a rod that will work for you.

Pick and Match to the Fish and to the Water

You wouldn't buy a Corvette to take deer hunting, and you wouldn't buy an Xterra to enter in a 500-mile road race. Each vehicle is designed for a specific function. A four-wheel-drive vehicle will never be a road racing car and shouldn't be used as one. The same is true for fly rods. What are you going to use your new rod for? No single rod will work for every species of fish or for every water situation. Think your needs through.

The first question you have to ask yourself is: *What kind of fish am I going to use this rod for?* Do you want a general, all-around rod, or do you want a rod designed for a specific fish? You wouldn't want to use a spring creek trout rod for big bass or a bluegill rod for bone fish. Nor would you want to use a salmon rod for pan fish.

This, in turn, may or may not answer the next question: *What kind of water am I going to be fishing on?* In addition to the species, what about the water conditions? If you are going to fish for trout on a small stream, you'll need a rod different from the one you use while casting for the same-size trout in a large river. Your rod, for example, might need to be longer and stiffer so you can effectively cast on larger waters. You may have to cast farther or throw more weight to get your wet fly deeper.

Another question might be: *Are there any other physical conditions that I need to consider?* For example, will you have to cast against a lot of wind? Is the current really strong or the water deep? In such cases you might need a longer or heavier rod.

Since most of us tend to be generalists, a middle-of-the-road rod is probably the best choice. Such a rod can do many things pretty well and handle the fringes in an acceptable manner. If you mostly fish for midsize trout in streams, rivers, and lakes, it would be silly to buy a heavy steelhead or bass fly rod. If you only fish bass a few days a year, you can easily make do with your general rod. It may not be perfectly designed for bass, but it'll work just fine when you use it.

For most of us, a general rod in the weight sizes #5 to #7 will be about right (a #5 being lighter, a #7 being heavier). If you are after bigger fish, go with a little heavier-weight rod like the #6 or #7. If you'll be on large bodies of water, casting a long way, or casting in the wind, you'll find a heavy rod is a more logical choice. If you're on small streams or need a more delicate, clear-water presentation, you'll be happier with a lighter-weight rod like a #5. (You will find the rod weight marked right above the handle.) You will need to match the line to the rod. This allows you to cast better since the line and rod are

Dave has just landed a nice bass at a local pond. Warm water fishing, especially for bass, requires that you use a heavier, stiffer rod so you can set the hook and turn the fish in structure.

The place to start is with a good rod and a good fly line.

balanced for each other. If you use the wrong line, you might be able to cast for short distances, but the line won't load nor will you cast well.

The length of the rod is another consideration. For most of us, an 8-foot-6 or a 9-foot rod is the right length. If, on the other hand, you are fishing in mostly bushy areas, you might want to go to a shorter rod: 7-foot-6 to 8-foot-6. But if you are going to fish lakes, from a boat or a float tube, you might want to consider a 9-foot to 9-foot-6 rod; the extra length will give you a casting edge on larger waters.

For the average person, a #5, #6, or #7 rod 9 feet long would be our suggestion. It will handle almost any fishing situation.

If you are the sort who wants to fish only for bass, steelhead, or spring creek trout or who plans to follow the salmon runs, you'll probably want a specialized rod.

For a full-time bass caster, a #7 to #8 rod will serve you well. Most favor the #8. Bass are thick, heavy-bodied fish that put a lot of stress on the rod and line; in addition, they are hard to turn. A heavy rod will be to your advantage. Also, bass flies are heavy and can be more effectively cast with a heavier line and rod. Lastly, when you do get hung up on trees, rocks, weeds, or the bottom, and every person fishing for bass frequently will, you can horse the rod and line.

Stripers, steelhead, and salmon are big, heavy fish that hang out in deep water or water that often has a lot of current and structure. You have to turn these freshwater lunkers and keep them from running downstream or under a fallen log. If you don't, you'll probably lose the fish. An angler has to have a heavy-enough rod to handle such situations. A #8 or #9 rod will be a must. (The best length would be 9 feet, 6 inches.) If the fish you're hunting are really heavy, or you're after Alaskan kings, we'd recommend at least a #9 or a #10.

For limestone creeks or spring creeks, or wherever the trout are really spooky, the word is *delicate*. You'll have to have a light, perfect presentation. You'll need a dainty rod that can cast a lighter line with a hairlike tippet. A #3 or #4 rod from 8 to 9 feet long will fill the bill since you'll rarely be casting more than 50 feet.

But to repeat for the benefit of the puzzled beginner: For the average person, a #5 to #7 rod 9 feet long will adequately handle just about anything.

Shopping for the Rod

Now that you have an idea about what you need, how do you make the selection? The first thing most of us think about is *price*. Price is a major consideration, but it can't be the only factor. You have to decide what is realistic for you to spend. If you go too cheap, you'll be disappointed in seconds. If you go too expensive, you'll bust your budget. You'll have to discover a middle ground, but remember that you get what you pay for.

Don't rush or get talked into anything. Take your time. So what if it takes a few days to find a rod. Go on a window-shopping spree and look at a lot of different rods. You now have an idea about the

Michael catching a bass. If you plan to fish in a float tube, you might want to consider a 10-foot rod—it will help you cast longer distances.

Your rod is your single most important fly casting investment. You can tell a rod's vital statistics by looking at the writing near the handle. The manufacturer's name, of course, will be boldly printed. VT2 in this case is the type of rod. Also the rod weight, a #3-weight, and rod length, 7.9 feet.

length and weight you'd like. Look at a number of rods in your desired size and weight. Take the rod out of the rack. False-cast with it. Assemble it and disassemble it. Does it feel like a long, thin, limp branch? When you shake it, does it keep shaking when you stop or does it damp quickly? Generally, the better rods recover quickly. You won't be happy with a piece of branch—nor will you be able to cast very far.

You'll probably rule out both the cheapest *and* the most expensive rod.

Do you want to go with an effective entry-level rod and upgrade later? Or do you want to throw caution to the wind and get a really good rod now and grow into it? There are pros and cons each way.

If you go with a good entry-level rod, you are spending some money, but you know you'll out-grow your rod sooner or later. As you become an intermediate fly caster, you may no longer be entirely satisfied with your casting—especially if you borrow a really good rod and see how pleasant it is. There is no shame in outgrowing a rod. At the same time, you'll discover enough about yourself and the sport to know what you want when you upgrade, thus purchasing a rod you can have for a long time and stay happy with.

If you buy a very good rod to start with, how-ever, you can grow into it. It's also a lot easier to cast with good equipment, and you'll pick up cast-ing faster. On the other hand, the beginning stage is sometimes clumsy and hard on equipment. And what if you spend $600 on a #4, 8-foot-6-inch rod and discover what you really wanted was a #6, 9-foot rod? If you decide to buy a good rod at first, make sure you think your decision through carefully so you get the right one—and don't end up wanting another later.

At Dave's casting schools, what to buy is a con-stant question. His recommendation, unless you're really sure what you want, is a *good* entry-level rod that will last you through the intermediate stages.

This is a rod you plan to outgrow, but it's a rod good enough to learn on and a rod good enough to use as your backup or loaner. This rod should keep you happy at least six months to a year—maybe more. When you feel you are in control, when you feel your current rod is holding you back from the kind of fishing you want to do, then upgrade. The better the entry-level rod you buy, the longer you'll be happy with it.

There are a number of fine rod manufacturers to choose from. Most make first-rate entry-level and intermediate rods. Redington, for example, makes a durable rod for a little over a hundred dollars with a lifetime guarantee. Michael and Dave have both seen a lot of life out of their Redingtons—rods that are fifteen years old and have caught plenty of fish. Perhaps the best bang for the casting buck is a rod made by Orvis. For the beginner, the Orvis Streamline, costing about $90, is probably the best deal in town. The Streamline is a great little rod made from a graphite blank, chrome guides, and aluminum reel seats. It also has a great guarantee. For casters on a tight budget, this is a good place to start.

Sage, G. Loomis, and Redington, among others, make noteworthy intermediate rods, and you can't go wrong with any of them. Mike and Dave have vintage Sage and G. Loomis entry-level rods that are still being used by their children. However, nowadays we think the best rod for the money is a little sleeper called the Clearwater by Orvis. You can take the Clearwater home for $150 (considerably less than most rods in its class, but you don't sacrifice performance). This is a great buy and a great rod. This rod has a crisp feel and casts smoothly. It also has a twenty-five-year guarantee.

A good rod will serve you well as you start. Some you'll outgrow faster than others. Go to your favorite fly shop and see which rod fits you best. While we both have young families and understand budgets and braces, price isn't the only consideration. Get a rod that feels good to you. If you travel or

Your rod, reel, and line stand between you and a trophy-size fish.

Dave's son is holding a striper bass—he has enough gear to handle a fish considerably larger.

If you do a lot of traveling, consider getting a rod that separates into four pieces. It will be a lot easier to transport.

backpack, consider a four-piece rod. It costs a little more but more than pays for itself in convenience.

If you know you love fly casting and you want a really excellent rod to begin with, consider a high-end rod that will take you from beginner to intermediate to expert. Consider manufacturers like Sage, G. Loomis, Thomas and Thomas, Orvis, Powell, or Winston. Each of these companies makes a superior rod, a rod you can use for the rest of your life.

A crafted rod does come with a price tag, but it will be a joy to fish with. We tried about every rod, and we have our favorites. For years, Michael fished almost exclusively with Sage and still considers the Sage XP and his old RPL among his favorite rods. Dave has always been partial to G. Loomis and Powell.

However, after trying most every rod under the sun, we'd be hard pressed to pick a single, perfect, across-the-board rod. There are so many good ones to choose from. For Michael the Sage XP would be close. Dave is more equivocal. Nevertheless, if we did have to pick one rod, it would be a casting instrument from the Zero Gravity Rod lineup by Orvis. Mike's comment when he borrowed a buddy's rod was, "This is the most responsive, perfectly timed rod I've ever used . . . bar none. I feel like I'm floating when I cast this rod." It took Dave hours before he could talk Michael into giving it back to our friend Steve.

More than a decade ago, Michael fished with the same Sage RPL #5 for many years. Dave figured Mike might have logged more than 600 days with that rod. He has switched to a Sage XP #5 now, using the RPL as a loving backup. Remember, you get what you pay for. Look for a good brand. We've had excellent luck with Hodgman. Orvis and Cabella's also sell quality products.

"Sure, Sage or Orvis is expensive," Mike says, "but I like how a good rod feels, and I'm willing to pay for it. You can fish a lifetime with a great rod. Buy it when you're a boy and get buried with it sixty years later.

"So far this RPL has cost a lot less than fifty cents a day to fish on—and I'll be using it for the next thirty years. I'm willing to pay to get this kind of performance." Remember, your rod makes or breaks your fly fishing experience.

Once you buy your rod, take good care of it.

If the statistics are right, rods usually don't get broken fighting large fish—it's usually the stupid things that trash them. Car doors and such will be the offenders. Dave has broken only two rods in his fishing career. Michael is a different story: He averaged a rod a year until he went to four-piece units. (Michael also trips a lot more.) Get used to putting your rod away at the end of the fishing day. Always store it in a good case. Wipe it down and clean it with furniture polish after each trip.

The Reel Thing

A reel is a place to hang good fly line.

If you want, you can spend enough on a reel that would be the equivalent of buying a good used compact car or a Rolex watch. Or you can spend what it would cost to take a friend to lunch at a third-rate steak house. Either way, the probability is very good that both reels would last and function without a hitch (though cheaper reels have more plastic, and the pawls wear out more quickly). But at this stage, almost any reel will do. There are a number of excellent manufacturers—and nowadays almost every rod manufacturer also sells reels. We're fond of Ross Reels, Cortland, Cabelas, Okuma, Redington, and Sage.

The Choices

There are several reel styles you should be aware of:

Pawl-Click Reels

This is the workhorse reel for most casters and is a good one to consider. You can spend about $30 to

You can expect years of performance out of a good reel.

A fly-reel design is simple.

A large arbor reel, like this Sage, weighs only three ounces and is a fine addition to your fishing lineup. Notice how much larger the spool is.

A large arbor reel has a number of advantages, one of which is the ability to reel line in faster. In simple terms, it means you get your fly in and out faster. That means more fishing time, which means more fish.

$100. The reel is very simple. A pawl finger, which fits into a gear, creates tension and slows down the line. The system is time tested and works well except for large fish, where a more even drag becomes important. If you open one of these reels, you'll see a large circular gear, the pawl, and a few other attachments. You could tear the whole thing apart in seconds—and so can a fish! Try to get a reel that's counterbalanced.

Disc Reels

This style of reel works like disc breaks on a car. This reel is a little more complicated than the pawl-click, but it's nothing like a spinning reel. Instead of applying pressure on one section (like the pawl), the pressure (drag) is applied evenly and more uniformly. This drag system is more dependable and smoother. And as you'd expect, there is less spool wobble. If you plan to fish for steelhead, salmon, or big trout, you ought to consider a disc reel because you need a good drag. The disadvantage is cost. A disc reel will cost from $75 to $400. The advantage is that this reel will last a lifetime and can be a joy to use.

Large Arbor Reels

In the last decade, large arbor reels have become increasingly more popular. Plainly put, large arbor reels have a much larger spool base.

These types of reels are especially useful when one is stripping out a lot of line or angling for fish that will take a lot of runs. You'll find large arbor reels among casters after large fish, especially salt-water species—you'll also find these reels used by salmon, bass, and steelhead anglers.

There are several advantages with this style of reel. There is higher line speed on recovery. In other words, you can reel the line in faster because the spool base is larger. There is also less line memory for better distance casting—the coils aren't so tight. And last of all, the drag is more consistent when a fish is stripping out line.

Multiplying Reels

In some fishing situations, you'll want to pick up line off the water rather quickly: a charging fish like a steelhead or salmon coming at you or a fish like a bass going for the bottom of the boat. If these are problems for you, you may want to consider a multiplying reel since it has a 2:1 ratio. This means you will get two revolutions of the spool for one turn of the handle. The cost is $50 to $350. The disadvantage is there are a lot of moving parts in these reels, and things can mess up.

Automatic Reels

Very few of these are now in use. They have a poor drag. Their only claim to fame is quick line retrieval. This reel, however, won't hold up to much pressure. No self-respecting caster would use an automatic reel. Don't consider one.

What to Look For

Get a reel that fits your budget.

Look for a reel that fits on your rod nicely and is somewhat light (although to get *really* light you have to *really* pay). Even if you do have a pawl-click reel, you still have a second drag—your palm. *Make sure your reel has an exposed spool* so you can "palm it." Most reels nowadays have the spools exposed—but not all. Double check. "If you can't palm it, you don't want it." As the line is being stripped out, you gently apply pressure to the exposed spool to slow down the fish. Any of the manufacturers we've suggested will provide you with a reel that can last a lifetime. Note that a lighter reel will give your rod a better balance. And, if you select a lightweight rod, you will defeat its purpose if your reel is too heavy.

Also, be sure to buy at least one extra spool. If you can't get them, don't buy the reel. It's better to have an inexpensive reel with several spools than a good reel without extras. You'll often be fishing with several different lines; it's essential to success. It's

When you buy a reel, buy an extra spool to go with it. An extra spool, with a different fly line on it, gives you a lot of casting versatility.

A reel is a great place to hold your line. Michael has used this System 2 reel for years without a problem. It has a disc drag, which is very handy if you catch a fish that wants to run with your line.

The line you select is your most important purchase after your rod. Michael caught this salmon with his good friend and guide Jim Dunlevy near the mouth of the Rogue River in southern Oregon.

easy to carry a couple of spools, but it's a mess to carry a couple of reels. Buy the extra spools when you buy your reel. No matter how good the reel is, it will eventually be discontinued, and then you won't find a spool for it anywhere.

The reel is a house for your valuable line. Don't get talked into spending a lot of your hard-earned dollars on an expensive unit. Sink that money into a rod and line instead. Move up to a better reel, like the System 2 disc reel, later when you know more about what you want from your equipment. Most of us have used the pawl-click reels with good success for years.

A Good Catchy Line

Next to your rod, your fly line is the single most important element in your tackle. The function of the fly line is simple: The weight of the line casts the fly. Like everything else, with lines you'll get what you pay for. *Don't go with a cheap line.*

A good line costs a few bucks, but it will last for quite a while and do you proud. Nothing stands between you and the fish of your dreams but your fly line (and, of course, your leader). Companies such as Scientific Anglers, Cortland, and Rio are some of the largest line manufacturers, and you can't go wrong with their products. They make lines for every experience level and for every type of casting.

It makes sense to take good care of your line, but you don't have to be compulsive about it. Short of nicks from a saber-toothed rock, a line will take a lot of abuse—and you can give it a lot of abuse if you're inclined.

Michael bought a Scientific Anglers WF-5-F line in 1991. He used the same line until the summer of 1996. He never cleaned it, he rarely rinsed it, and he got it dirty and muddy countless times fishing for bass or spring trout.

There are a lot of lines out there. We often fish with Cortland and Scientific Anglers lines, however, and see no reason to change. A good line is an investment in your sport. It will last a long time if you take care of it.

Line Weight

A fly line is heavy and has body. The action of the rod moves it. The line moves the leader and thus the fly. As you would expect, a #3 fly line is lighter and has less body than a #8. The weight (numbers) of the line actually means how many grams the first 30 feet of line weighs. And as you'd expect, it takes a stiffer, more powerful rod to throw a #8 line than a #3 line. When you cast a spinning rod, the flex of the rod and the weight of the lure do the casting. The line is just along for the ride. But when you fly cast, the line does all (or most) of the work.

The reason an angler fishing a spring creek might demand a #3 or #4 rod and line is presentation. Because the line is light, it can be cast so it floats like a snowflake and doesn't scare the fish. It's hard, if not impossible, to get a #8 line to drop with the airy presentation of a #3. Long leaders will help in a delicate presentation, but they are much harder to cast.

As you would expect, the rod weight and line weight are matched. A #5-weight rod will only take #5-weight line, a #8 rod will only take #8 line, and so forth. If you change lines of one weight with rods of another weight, you are asking for trouble. This is one reason why you need to determine your fishing needs before investing in a rod/line system. It's expensive to change. Some rods list two weights, such as #7/#8. You're usually better off going with a higher line weight. Higher-end rods will handle one line weight higher than is listed on the rod—but you'll be better off staying within the manufacturer's recommendations.

There are a number of different fly lines available. Match the fly line to your rod. WF-4-F on the box means Weight Forward, for a 4 weight rod, Floating Line.

Buying tapered leader is a lot easier than tying a leader up by hand—and there are no knots to break or catch the moss.

The Nail Knot

Attaching fly line to leader

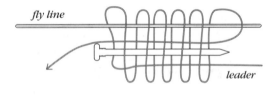

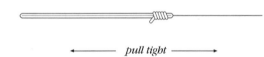

← *pull tight* →

Remember: *Match the right line weight to the rod.*

Line Taper

There's more than just line weight when we consider lines. You'll have to make another decision: What sort of line taper do you want?

By taper, we mean the shape of the fly line or the shape of one part of the fly line.

You'll need to ask yourself some of the same questions you asked when you selected a rod. What kind of fish am I after? What kinds of conditions will I be fishing under? What kind of casting am I going to do?

There are many different tapers. The main ones are *Level Taper, Weight Forward, Double Taper,* and *Shooting Head Taper.* Each has advantages and disadvantages.

Level Taper. The L taper is a straight line. Every part of the line has the same diameter. The only advantage to this line is that it's cheap. It has no advantages otherwise, and we recommend that you not use it.

Weight Forward. As the name implies, there is more weight on the front part of this line—a larger diameter—making it easier to cast. The main weight of the line is forward. The WF line is easy to cast, and it loads well. Michael feels it's the best line for beginner and expert alike because it's the most forgiving and it shoots smoothly. WF can be a little more expensive than double taper line, however, and isn't quite as delicate. Unlike the double taper line, when you wear the WF line out you can't reverse it and have a new line.

Double Taper. As the name implies, both ends of the line are tapered, and it's heavy in the middle. In the long run, DT line is certainly cheaper since you really have two lines. When you first start casting, you do a lot of practicing, and this can be hard on

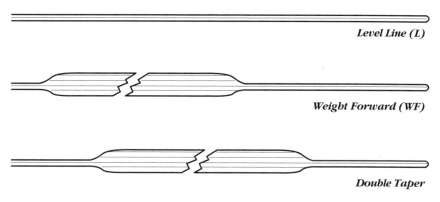

Level Line (L)

Weight Forward (WF)

Double Taper

The Three Basic Lines

line—especially if you hit concrete, pavement, or rocks. When you wear one side of your line out, as you will if you practice much, all you have to do is reverse the ends, and you have a new line. This is also a good line for stack or mend casts. Although Michael recommends the WF line for beginners, Dave recommends the DT: It's cheaper in the long run, and the performance is excellent. A DT will perform better than the WF at short distances—a nice thing to know, since most fish are caught within 40 feet.

Shooting Head Taper. With this line system, you change the "head" of the line and put on another: You change heads to meet the requirements of the cast and the conditions. With this system, you can get long casts, and you don't have to carry several spools loaded with line—only different heads. This is something you should be aware of at this stage of your casting, but this isn't the right choice for your first line. Wait until you have more of the loose ends worked out.

Two things to always remember about line:
• Buy a floating line
• Match the line weight to the rod

GPX is a great all-purpose line. It has a subtle coating to help reduce memory, advanced floating properties, and great "shootability." The line is a great bargain. It comes in Double Taper (DT) and Weight Forward (WF). We recommend starting with a WF.

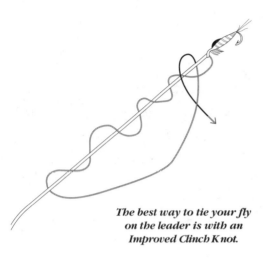

*The best way to tie your fly
on the leader is with an
Improved Clinch Knot.*

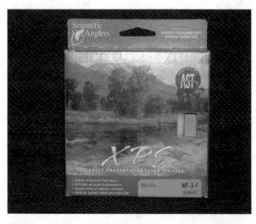

*XPS is a fine line for cold water and spring creeks. It
has a supple coating to reduce memory. The subtle
taper on the front allows you to cast with precision.*

Line Action

Now that we've learned about line taper, let's look at what is meant by *line action*.

Put another way, *what does the line do?* Lines are built to perform in different ways.

The action of the line means it either floats or sinks—or sinks to some prescribed degree.

In the old days, a fly line was made of braided horse hair or cotton string. Later it was an expensive piece of silk. If you covered your silk with floatant, the line floated. As the floatant wore off, or if you applied only a small amount of floatant, it would slowly sink. If you didn't apply any floatant to your line, it would sink quickly as soon as it was water-logged. All in all, casting was difficult and messy. Obviously, it was hard to switch from wet to dry or dry to wet. Line also required a lot of care, or it would rot.

With modern fly lines, science has taken out a lot of the frustration. Now it is possible to buy a fly line that does anything you want. This is why we recommended you purchase several spools. With an extra spool or two, you can cover just about any fishing situation you might encounter by simply popping on another line.

Some of the line actions you should be acquainted with are *Floating (F), Sinking (S), Sinking Tips (ST), Sink Tip Systems,* and *Uniform Sink.* Each of these lines does a different job for different fishing conditions.

Floating Line. Your first line should be a floating line. This is the best day-in, day-out line for most people. Most fishing conditions can be met with a floating line, and it's easy to pick up, an important factor when you're mastering the sport. If you do need to get your fly under the surface, you can use a weighted fly or weight the line. You'll likely use a floating line at least 75 percent of the time. The floating line should be your first investment.

Sinking Line. A sinking line, as the name implies, sinks. Yes, you can weight a floating line.

But you can only go so deep, and it's difficult to cast with split shot. You'll reach diminishing returns. When this happens, you need a line that will get your fly down. Depending on what you want, there are different sinking lines that sink at different speeds. After a floating line, a sinking line will probably be your next choice. If you are fishing in deep rivers, ponds, or lakes where the fish are down there, this line is a must. Some lines sink quickly and are useful where there is a swift current or you are fishing deep. Other lines sink at intermediate levels. Some lines sink very slowly. Your first sinking line should be an intermediate one since it's the most versatile.

Sinking Tips. With this line, only the tip—not the entire body—of the line sinks. This line is very useful for steelhead or salmon where the water is heavy and you need to get your fly to the fish. It is also useful to the tube fisher who wants to fish for trout suspended 5 to 10 feet under the film. This line helps when you don't need to go really deep, but you do have to get your fly down fast. The advantage with this line is that you still have the body floating on the water, so you can pick up or mend easily. The line is still very sensitive. Another advantage is that you can fish the subsurface effectively by stripping the fly, retrieving the fly in small jerks or "strips," and still have some visible contact with the floating line.

Sink Tip Systems. This system allows a caster to attach a sinking "head" to the line. You can get different degrees of sinkability depending on which head you chose. Instead of carrying different sinking lines, you carry different heads and attach them as needed.

Uniform Sink Line. This line sinks in a straight line so you have uniform contact with the fly. This way when the fish takes the fly, you can feel it because there's no discrepancy, no gap between line, leader, and fly. When you set the hook, you don't have to take up a lot of slack line.

Dave is holding a bottom fish he caught in the Gulf of Alaska on his fly rod. The right line is essential for success. He is using a sinking line and a heavy leader.

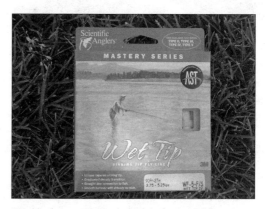

Wet Tip has a unique tapered tip for smooth turnovers. It is a great line for lake fishing.

Putting Your Money Down

Make sure you purchase a *good* line. Your fly line isn't the place to save a buck. Plan to spend around $40 to $60 on your first line. You can buy a fly line a lot cheaper, but you'll be disappointed in the long run. You won't have the control you'd like, so your cast will suffer. Conversely, you can spend $50 or more, but for now that would be a waste of money.

Go with a good middle-of-the-road line. Our recommendation would be the Scientific Anglers Air Cell Supreme Headstart Line or the Cortland 333. This is a good line for the newcomer or the person who fishes only every so often. This line will make casting less complicated because you can load your line easily and the line and leader don't pile up readily. And the slightly bulkier tip is more elevated in the water, making it easier to see the line telegraph when a fish hits.

Backing

The backing on the line connects your fly reel to your fly line. The backing is very important. If you get a big fish on, the fly line itself usually isn't long enough to play the fish. You'll need more line so the fish can run and wear itself out—not snapping the fragile leader in the process—and that's where the backing comes in. A really big fish doesn't happen often enough, but when it does, you'll be glad you're backed up. Sometimes you'll get into your backing on intermediate-size fish. Once Dave hooked a three-pound brown that decided on a whim to take off downstream a few miles. Within seconds, the feisty fish stripped off his fly line and a third of the backing. Dave ran like a madman to catch up with the runner and finally was able to net this ambitious brown—thanks to a lot of backing. It was an exciting fifteen-minute ride. And this wasn't an overly large fish—it was just scrappy.

After doing battle with a big fish, you'll be glad you have backing. Rarely is your fly line more than a hundred feet—certainly not long enough to turn a large fish! Every reel should have a lot of backing.

Another reason for backing is that it fills out the extra room in your spool and keeps the loops of your valuable fly line loose. It also increases your line pickup by increasing the spool diameter.

Buy a spool of backing when you buy your line. The day you fish without backing is the day you'll hook the biggest fish of your career. And for the biggest fish of your life, you'll need backing. It's not expensive—in fact, it's cheap insurance.

To get the backing and fly line balanced properly on the reel, wind your fly line on the reel first, then wind on the backing until it's 1/4 inch from the lip of the reel. Next, take the backing off, then the fly line. Now attach the backing to the reel and wind it on. Then attach the fly line to the backing and wind it on. Nowadays, you can usually find information on how much backing to use on the box or the instruction sheet that comes with your reel.

Leader

You'll grow into your leader. And as you fish, you'll discover the type of leader that works best for you.

When you first start casting, a leader is just a tapered line—anything will do. After a while, you begin to see the subtle, then not-so-subtle differences among brands. Leaders frankly have personalities. They've gotten somewhat specific these days, different fish requiring different styles. Dave leans toward the Umpqua leader, while Michael is partial to the Frog Hair leaders.

After you've started to get your cast and presentation worked out, a certain brand of leader will likely appeal to you. We both favor a very soft leader with little memory (with the exception of bass fishing or some types of nymphing).

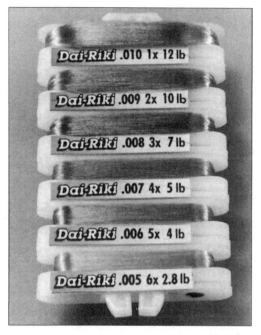

The end of your leader, called the tippet, wears out as you tie on flies. Instead of replacing the leader, a caster carries various tippet materials of differing pound-test lines. This leader caddy is a handy way of carrying extra lines that are instantly accessible and easy to adjust for different situations.

There are a number of good leaders and tippets to choose from. Most casters need to experiment with different brands until they settle on a favorite.

It's hard to do without a good pair of waders—especially in cold weather. You can stay warm wearing long johns, blue jeans, and several pair of socks.

Just Wading Around

You may not need waders at first, but before too long you'll want a set. Waders expand your fishing season and increase your percentages. Some fly casting can be done from the bank, and in the summer you can wade in tennis shoes, but this is limiting.

The truth is that most effective fly casting requires some wading. Even in the summer the water is cold, so your stay in the water is limited. For the serious fly caster, waders are a must.

You get what you pay for with waders. Buy a good set, and you'll get years of use out of them.

Michael and Dave have both used Hodgman for years. Michael has had the same set forever. They fit him like an old glove. He's had them since 1981, when he was in graduate school. They have plenty of patches by now, and even though he finally bought a new pair, he still uses the old ones as loaners.

Michael is either frugal or he's downright cheap, since this is only the third pair of neoprene waders he's owned. Michael figures they cost him less than eight dollars a year. Dave, on the other hand, has had a dozen pair of waders—he has a thing about tearing shirts and waders. The truth, however, is this: A less expensive set will have to be replaced a lot sooner than a high-quality pair. A high-quality pair will also be easier to repair.

A last piece of advice regards wader thickness. If you have to err, we suggest you err on the side of thickness. If you do much fishing in the winter, you'll be pleased when the weather gets nippy. You'll fish a lot longer. If you get cold easily, get 5 mm waders.

Any wader is going to be hot if you have to walk very far. If you have to go very far, it's better to lace up a pair of running shoes. In the long haul, you'll be a lot more comfortable. We learned this at the Green River in eastern Utah. The fishing was great, but you needed to walk a mile or so from the truck to escape the crowd. We packed our waders, walked from the madding crowds, and in no time were catching lots of fish.

Even in spring or autumn weather, a mile hike is quite warm. It's a lot better to walk to where you have to go and put your waders on there.

Wader Types

Look at the kind of fishing you are going to do the most. There isn't a perfect wader system. Match the wader to the water you fish in. Waders can be broken down into two categories: *chest waders* and *hip waders.*

Chest Waders. Chest waders are the logical choice for most of us because they can do anything a hip wader can do, and more. You can use chest waders in a float tube or for wading a stream, river, lake, or pond. You can wade up past your waist with relative comfort and safety. You won't have as many nasty surprises when you're fishing in chest-high waders. In a creek or river, it's easy to misjudge the depth and have water gurgle in over the top of your hippers. Chest waders are, however, a bit cumbersome to walk in. If you have to hike very far to get to your fishing area, you'd be advised to take them off and carry them on your back. Hiking in chest waders is sweaty business. Hip waders are a lot cooler, and walking isn't problematic.

Hip Waders. With hip waders, you have to be careful that you only go in water that is mid-thigh deep. This is easier said than done. Some streams are so clear they look about a foot deep. The reality is you might go in over your head. If you're not very careful, testing uncertain steps first, you'll have water gushing in your waders unless the top leg strap is tightly secured. Murphy has a law about wearing hip waders: Every time you cross a stream, one part will be exactly 2 inches higher than the tops of your boots. On the bright side, hip waders are comfortable and much cooler than chest waders. When you walk, you can loosen the safety strap or

A good pair of hip waders will allow you to fish streams that aren't very deep. Hip waders are also a good way to fish when you have to walk a ways, as they aren't as hot as chest waders.

Mike's daughter, Abbey, would bring him his waders when he was about to hit the Provo River with Dave. It was her way of begging to come along; it's now a family joke. She has her own waders these days, and, yes, she still holds them out when she wants to go fish.

drop the top part of the boot down around your knees. For most spring creeks and smaller streams, a hip wader is a wonderful thing. If you have to walk very far, especially in swampy and boggy terrain, this is an excellent boot. We've been to Alaska a number of times and have lived in hip waders for weeks on end. (Except for Dave's athlete's foot, everything worked quite well.)

Sooner or later you'll end up with both hip waders and chest waders. However, the chest waders are our general recommendation.

Basically, there are three kinds of materials waders are made from: *rubber, neoprene,* and *a breathable material like Supplex or Gore-Tex*.

Rubber Waders. This is the cheapest way to go, and such waders work pretty well. You can get a set of hip waders from $20 and chest waders from $30. The advantage, besides price, is that they go on quickly and can be patched easily if you tear them. They are cool and very abrasion resistant. There are a few drawbacks: Rubber waders frequently don't fit well because there's no stretch. They are generally loose, and thus there's more drag in the water—a real disadvantage when you're in a float tube or wading in deep water with a current. A year's worth of use is about all you'll get from a cheap pair before the rubber starts to crack and split. You can get a few years out of a more expensive pair. If you store your waders without folding them and apply an occasional coat of Armor All, you can increase their life considerably.

Neoprene Waders. These probably offer the best bang for the buck. They stretch, they fit snugly, and there is little water drag. Because of this, such a wader is safer and is the only choice for someone who will be using a float tube or wading in heavy rivers. Also, when you do take a plunge, and it happens to everyone now and then, you'll notice that neoprene is more buoyant.

Since neoprene hugs your body, these waders aren't as likely to fill up with water the way baggy

Neoprene stocking-foot waders. You have to have a pair of boots, too.

rubber waders are prone to do. Neoprene feels like a wet suit and is very flexible and comfortable. It moves and bends with you. Neoprene will tear, but it's simple to patch. In colder conditions, neoprene is warmer than rubber because it insulates. In warmer conditions, it's hot. In the long run, this wader will be more economical since it lasts a long time. A set of these waders will set you back from $70 to $250. You can get a really good pair that will last for years for more than $100. When you purchase your waders, also buy a tube of repair material.

Breathable Waders. To quote Mike, "Breathable waders are one of the finest inventions since the laptop." Unlike the neoprene wader, which is heavy and warm, the breathable wader is light and supple—and comfortable. These waders are made with Gore-Tex or Supplex (or some similar material). The laminate is both waterproof and breathable, providing a comfortable fit. Usually there are neoprene booties that prevent bunching up in the wading boots. While breathable waders are thin and cool in the summer, you can make them comfortable and warm for winter wear with good long underwear and fleece pants.

Except when it gets very cold, about all we wear these days are Hodgman Breathables. Price varies on these waders: The more you pay, the longer you can expect them to last. Consider getting a reinforced knee. We love breathable waders, but it's important to buy a good brand. Stick with the two giants in the industry, Hodgman and Orvis.

Lightweight "breathable" Supplex waders.

Built-In Boots and Wading Boots/Shoes

Some waders have a built-in boot; others have a stocking foot and you have to buy a boot to wear over it. The advantage of a wader with a built-in boot is that you can get in and out of it fast. You don't have to fiddle with laces and such. Most rubber waders come with a built-in boot. Most

A wading boot that goes over stocking-foot waders. Before you buy boots, see how they fit over your waders.

Take a repair kit for your waders on fishing trips. You'll be glad you did. Nylon or rubber waders are very easy to patch. Neoprene waders can be patched, too.

If you have waders or boots that don't have felt soles, you can wear a felt slipover for greater stability.

neoprene waders will have "stocking feet," and you'll still have to buy the boot.

If a boot is built into the wader, the fit will tend to be generic—a little loose and sloppy or too tight. It's better to have the wader a little loose. You customize the fit by adjusting the number of socks. Be careful when buying a wader to ensure that the built-in boot will be comfortable. At the least, take a light pair of socks and a few heavy pairs along with you to see if you can get a good fit.

A pair of wading boots will run you from $50 to $100. The combination of stocking waders and boots is more expensive up front than rubber waders with built-in boots, but in the long run they won't be any more costly than replacing rubber waders a time or two. The question is, do you want to pay now or pay later? Only you can answer that.

The stocking-footed wader has become very popular because it permits you to buy a boot that gives you a sure grip when wading. You can buy a boot that actually fits so that your feet don't move about when you are working your way over rocks in tough currents. The generic fit presented in a booted wader isn't always comfortable. But with a wading boot or shoe, you can have a product that fits you well. If you have to walk a long way to fish, a well-fitting boot is a plus. In addition, a boot can be removed when you fish in a float tube so that you can slip on a flipper. (A flipper over a boot is a lot of drag.)

There are a number of good companies to select from—we recommend Hodgman because they stand behind their products and they make good quality affordable. If you are on a budget, Hodgman makes an excellent boot. We have used Hodgman boots for years

When you buy a boot, take your waders with you. In theory, you buy your wading boot according to your shoe size. But the thickness of waders often varies. Try the boot on with your waders and a thick pair of socks. Your wading boot should fit snugly, but it should be comfortable.

It's critical that your wading shoes be comfortable. If they're too tight, your feet will feel cold. If they aren't comfortably snug, you'll lose your balance.

Always choose a *felt sole* for your wading boots. The felt sole will give you good footing on slippery bottoms and moss-covered rocks. If the felt soles are studded, that will be fine. (The studs increase the life of the sole and give good support on rocks.) Yes, felt soles wear out. And the farther you have to walk to get to your favorite river, the quicker they'll go. But felt soles are easy to replace and are not expensive.

The felt soles on your waders/boots are easily replaced.

Safety Stuff

Few fly casters drown. But anytime you wade, there is an element of risk. Depending on the water, wading can be very safe or very dangerous. You should always use good judgment and know your limitations. No fish is worth a trip to Saint Peter. To help ensure your safety, please consider the following suggestions:

If you are on dangerous water, always fish with someone else and wear an inflatable safety vest. Dave saw a man lose his balance and get swept down the Kenai River in Alaska. He was a mile downriver before someone on a passing salmon fishing boat could grab him. The man was scared but kept his head. He was wearing an inflatable safety vest. He lost his rod and a little bit of dignity, but he was all right.

Everyone goes down now and then. Always wear a wading belt near the top of your chest waders. In case you take a tumble, this prevents water from filling your waders and pulling you under. *A wading belt is a must for rubber chest waders!* A wading belt also is a good idea for neoprene chest waders, even

An inflatable vest like this Stearns could save your life.

Nothing is more rewarding than a day on the water with your kids. It's important, however, that you get your kids fly fishing equipment that fits them properly.

Winter fishing is exciting. Snow on the ground does not mean fishing is poor. If you fish in the winter, you need to dress very warmly and dress in layers.

though they are more snug and not as likely to fill with river water. A belt also keeps the air in your waders and helps you stay buoyant.

If you are fishing in dangerous water, consider a flotation device—either a noninflatable design or an inflatable model charged by a CO_2 cartridge (in which a CO_2 cartridge in the vest or in the suspenders inflates an air bladder). The man Dave saw on the Kenai River, a mighty powerful water, probably would have drowned if he hadn't had a safety vest on. In many states, if you are in a float tube or a boat, a flotation device is required by law.

If you are wading in heavy water, consider using a so-called third leg—a stick or staff to help you maintain balance. Some wading staffs break down and store in your vest.

Felt soles will do more to keep you off your fanny than any other single thing. Some folks use carpet glued to the bottom of their boots. This works better than nothing, but it's not as good as felt. To help keep your balance, you can also put wading chains over your felt soles. This will help you to keep your footing in rocky or rough areas.

Dress for Casting Success

Folks can get carried away on the dressing thing. Fly fishing isn't a fashion show, but on some very exclusive waters, you'd never know it. Most of us would rather sink money into gear. A trophy rainbow trout doesn't care if you are wearing designer duds, nor will a label on your shirt help you cast any better. Clothing is important, but it's not that important. You need to wear what's comfortable.

Sun Protection

The sun is no joke these days. We have a friend who is now casting at that big trout stream in the sky because he didn't take the proper sun precautions.

Skin cancer isn't a prank or a passing fancy. It's something we've all got to consider if we want to fish into our eighties. In the last decade sun-related cancer is up over 50 percent (depleting the ozone layer is no laughing matter).

We weren't careful when we were young and foolish: We'd get a good deep-water tan, maybe wear a hat (more for the glare), and let it go at that. By the end of the summer we'd look like well-tanned shoe leather. However, when you see the firsthand results of *el sol,* you get more careful. Doctors estimate that one in eighty-nine people will develop a sun-related skin cancer.

If you fish a lot, you're going to be exposed to a lot of sun—it's an occupational hazard. But it's a problem you can do something about.

The first thing you need to do is buy a bottle of SPF 30-plus sunscreen and use it—especially on your face, neck, and hands—or whatever parts are hanging out. By the way, SPF means sun protection factor. An SPF rating of 30 means the sunscreen will give you thirty times more protection from sunburn that you would have with bare skin. So, use lots of sunscreen and repeat the process every few hours. Also, wear a hat with a generous brim and consider wearing a very thin nylon-sleeve shirt (like the bone fly casters on the Keys are so fond of).

Hats

A good hat is a must. You want to keep off the rain and the sun. A good bill will help keep the sun out of your eyes and face and be useful in keeping you tuned on hunting for fish. There are a number of good fly fishing hats on the market that provide a long bill to cut the glare in front and flaps in back to keep the rays off your neck (and to help keep you from getting skin cancer). A dark underside on the bill will help cut the glare even more. A good baseball cap or a cowboy hat will work quite well.

A good hat is an important piece of fly-casting equipment. It will keep off the sun, the rain . . . and keep you warm.

A case like this makes carrying your equipment easy and more trouble free.

Carrying Arrangements: Fishing Vest vs. Fishing Pack

You've got to have something to carry all your equipment in.

Do you want to use a vest or a pack? A vest fits snugly and has a lot of handy pockets for your gear. A fishing pack should have handy pockets and some big cargo areas to carry more large fly boxes, rain jackets, lunch, and water.

We've used both with good success and see pros and cons with each. When you are starting out and don't have that much stuff, a vest seems to be a good choice since it's usually cheaper. After you start carrying a lot of stuff, a lot more than you will likely require, you need a backpack (or a Sherpa).

You need to look for several features in a vest or a pack. Look for a lot of pockets to store a lot of stuff. What you need should be right at your fingertips. The vest or pack should be comfortable and feel good. Remember, they all feel good when empty. Load some stuff in it and see how it rides. (Tell the clerk so he won't think you're shoplifting.) Save some larger cargo area in the back for lunch, canteen, raincoat, jacket. Sometimes when you load a vest too much, it gets more uncomfortable than a pack (which is designed for more weight).

You can spend from $15 to $200. There are a lot of good systems out there. Start off as cheaply as you can. For now you just need something to hold your stuff. After you've used it for a while, you'll have a better idea about what you want. Or you can be like Michael, who has never used the same vest or pack for longer than a month. He's still looking for the perfect system. Dave has used the same pack system for years.

Accessories Make the Outfit

This section will show the reason you need a vest or a pack. You'll need to carry around some fly fishing stuff to help make your new vocation as a caster easier.

Rain Gear

No matter where you live, rain is something every caster will deal with sooner or later. The Boy Scouts had something with their motto: Be Prepared.

If it doesn't rain all that often where you live, a cheap raincoat will likely do. It needs to be light, and you'll need to have it with you if you expect to stay dry. Most raincoats are left in camp or in a vehicle.

If you plan to fish in wet country, you may want to invest in a better raincoat/jacket. You obviously won't need rain pants since you'll probably be wearing waders. If you want to be comfortable and stay out in any kind of weather, you'd better have rain gear that works. Remember, fishing can be very good in the rain . . . if you're prepared to stay out.

You'd think buying a raincoat would be simple, but it isn't. There are about a hundred choices, and it's easy to get lost in the maze. To start with, some rainwear will be breathable but waterproof, and some will be fully waterproof but not breathable. It's a puzzle. Good, lightweight, breathable stuff, something a caster will consider, comes with a price tag. Jackets that are waterproof but not breathable are often reasonably priced, but they are either too heavy to carry or not sturdy enough to take the abuse a caster will give.

You get what you pay for with jackets that are waterproof and breathable. Not all Gore-Tex or similar stuff is created equal. We can say this since we've tried about every rain product on the market and have come to believe that the ad executives don't get out much these days.

We've both fished the rain forests of Alaska and western Canada. Michael is originally from Oregon (where being waterproof like a duck is a necessity). If you are going to buy breathable gear, go with a

Rain gear is a must. Both Dave and Michael think the Helly-Hansen is about the best "breathable" rain jacket on the market. It has tons of pockets and special sleeves that Velcro tight so you can dip your arm into the water to scoop up fish and not get your shirt wet.

Dave's son proudly holding his catch. Wearing his rain jacket, he was able to fish all day in a drizzle.

high-end product, or you're just wasting your money. Gore-Tex gets all the press, but there are a number of waterproof/breathable jackets. We've both been pretty wet in high-end Gore-Tex in a major all-day rain; we're not all that confident about it.

In our opinion, one of the best breathable/waterproof products is made by Helly-Hansen, and it's not Gore-Tex. Helly-Hansen's Deep Water Parka, for example, is a great product and, as far as we're concerned, is the best thing out there. First of all, it works. You'll stay dry. And it's light, roomy, and has special cuffs that Velcro shut so you can dip a hand into the water and not get your shirt wet. It's the most practical thing we've seen. It's designed for the fly caster. As a point of interest, all the guides we encountered in Canada last year were wearing Helly-Hansen.

Most any nonbreathable rain jacket will shed rain, but look carefully at the weight factor. If it weighs too much, you'll be tempted to leave it in camp and not carry it with you. If you get a light nonbreathable jacket, it will be easy to carry, but it won't stand up to much abrasion.

We always carry a disposable rain poncho in our vests in case we get caught in a shower (they only cost a dollar and are as thin as a garbage bag). However, if it looks like rain, we carry our regular jackets in the back of our vests. A sudden shower or an all-day storm won't drive us away.

Nets

A net offers the best way to scoop up a fish.

Sometimes the use of a net is the only way to land a large trophy fish. It is an important tool. Since we often use a leader with a light tippet, getting a fish in can be quite a trick. When you have the fish out some distance, the flexibility of the rod will cushion the fragility of the leader. But when you get the fish in close, the pressure is more direct. If you can slip your net under the fish, you don't have to

A net can be an important tool. Make sure your net's basket is made of soft cotton so it won't hurt the fish.

struggle grabbing it (thus straining and often snapping the tippet).

Another good reason for a net is getting to the fish quickly so you don't stress it. If you plan to release the fish, you'll want to get it back into the water as quickly as you can. A net speeds up the process. Always use a net with a cotton basket. It's much easier on the fish.

Another plus for a net: If you fish in cold weather, a net keeps your hands out of the water and thus keeps them warmer. Regardless of how you attach your net to your vest, be sure you can get to the net one-handed.

Kit Necessities

There are some things you need to carry with you at all times. These are things you can't do without: (We'll go into more detail about many of these items later.)

- *Fly box(es)* that hold a selection of flies.
- *Tapered leader* and small *spools of leader;* various sizes and lengths for different situations.
- *Fly floatant,* to be applied to your fly to keep it floating nicely on the surface.
- *Nippers,* to save your teeth. These are handy for clipping leader and tippet.
- *Hemostat,* for quickly removing a fly from a squirming fish.
- *Sinkers* in a variety of sizes, beneficial when trying to get a wet fly to bump across the bottom.
- *Strike indicators* for wet fly fishing. These are attached to the leader and act like a bobber so you'll know when a fish has picked up your fly.
- An original *Swiss Army knife* is the handiest all-purpose tool we've ever found for the fly caster. A model like the Champ, which Michael has carried for years, has a zillion features and a thousand uses—from tightening and repairing reels and equipment to cleaning fish and cutting line (and don't forget sawing branches or look-

A good knife is a must. We both carry a Victorinox Swiss Army knife. It keeps a razor edge and has a hundred uses.

ing at a bug with the magnifying glass). Michael has even skinned a bear with his knife. Dave likes the Fisherman model. There are countless uses for these knives, but beware: There are a lot of imitations that are next to useless. The "real" Swiss Army knife is made by Victorinox. And unlike cheap imitations (which fall apart quickly), the cutting blades on these knives hold a razor edge. This tool is a lifetime investment. You won't be sorry.

- *Polarized glasses,* absolutely critical if you like to catch fish. Since these glasses will cut the glare, you can see where the fish are holding, when fish are going for a fly, and where structure exists in the water. Plus, they'll keep you from getting a headache because of the glare. They'll also protect your eyes from branches or careless casts.

Other things you may want to consider carrying in the field:

- *Hook sharpeners,* because sharp hooks increase your fishing success by 25 percent.
- *Thermometer,* so you'll know the temperature of the water. You'll be more able to prepare for hatches and to judge fish behavior.
- *Insect net,* which will help you find out which bugs the fish are going for.
- *Stomach pump,* for identifying the hatch.
- *Gloves,* a nice addition.
- *Bear spray.* If you're fishing or camping in bear country, this is a must. Bear attacks are unlikely, but it's nice to have the added insurance. No spray is 100 percent effective, nor does it replace common sense, but it's good insurance. One summer in the Rockies, a friend of ours turned a sow grizzly at 10 feet with a dose of spray.
- *First-aid kit.* Stuff happens. If you don't carry one on your person, then at least have a first-aid kit in your car or camp. Adventure Medical Kits

Some rods come with a hard case. If your rod doesn't have a case, don't leave your favorite store without purchasing one. A rod without a hard case is soon to be a broken rod.

has a variety of kits for the outdoor person to choose from. We carry the Optimist, which is a small pouch that weighs six ounces. It fits easily into a vest or pack. It comes in very handy.

- *Rod case.* You spend a lot of money for your rod. Protect it. If your rod doesn't come with a tube or case, it's a good idea to get one. If you fish a lot or have a handy stream nearby, DP Dun makes an excellent case you can fit your rod into with the reel on. The Dun is one of the best buys on the market.

3

PUTTING YOUR BEST FLY FORWARD

Presentation of the Fly

Casting is the lifeblood of fly fishing.

It's what makes fly fishing special, artistic, and graceful. Indeed, it is a skill that you can hone and refine for the rest of your life. But "throwing line," as it's lovingly referred to, seems to be the major stumbling block when you first start.

Casting is a learned skill.

There are many things to consider, but casting is something you can do. You'll be a little self-conscious at first, but who isn't? The master caster will catch more fish than the novice, just as the master bowler will bowl more strikes than the apprentice. Nevertheless, the novice caster is going to catch fish (just as the novice bowler will roll some strikes).

Casting is the lifeblood of fly fishing. Casting isn't difficult—it just takes practice . . . and practice . . . and practice.

Differences between Spin Casting and Fly Casting

We've made a bold claim that anyone who can spin cast can fly cast. We'll stand by that observation. There are many similarities in the motion of casting. There are also a couple of differences we think you should be aware of.

The first difference is the line itself. In spin casting, the weight of the lure does the casting—the

Landing a good fish is the final result of a good cast.

Your grip on the rod is critical. Hold your thumb as shown here. Always hold the line with your index finger.

The Casting Clock

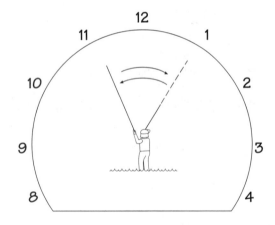

Pretend that you are casting next to a giant clock. The tip of the rod will travel back and forth between the eleven o'clock and the one o'clock positions.

line is mostly along for the ride. The spinner is concerned about getting the lure moving fast in order to pick up speed. But in fly fishing, the weight of the line does the casting—the fly is along for the ride. The fly caster is concerned with getting the line moving briskly.

While the arm motions for both casts have similarities, the movements are different. Spin casting is a sweeping arc, a half-circle motion (from three o'clock to nine o'clock). When you cast a fly, you paint a straight line with the tip of your rod (from eleven o'clock to one o'clock or one o'clock to eleven o'clock).

The Basic Cast: Getting the Line Out

The basic cast is the most important cast to master.

Nearly all the other casts we will talk about are variations on this standard classic. Don't worry if it doesn't come together perfectly at first. What you need to do is understand the basic motions. Then practice the steps.

Don't compare yourself to others. You are only competing against yourself. Making progress is all you are worrying about.

The Fly Caster's Grip

While it seems like a simple thing, the grip on a fly rod is very important and is a good place to start. The proper grip will help your cast and speed up your learning curve. As with golf or tennis, something as simple as grip can make or break your day.

Following are the steps in getting the right grip on the rod:

1. Pick up the rod.
2. Grip the cork (handle) so the reel is hanging down. Don't hold it too tightly. Hold it snugly.
3. Place your thumb so it is pointing up (to the top of the rod).

General Things to Remember

The first truth: *The line does what the rod tip tells it to do, and the rod tip does what your arm tells it to do.*

Remember: *The line follows the tip of the rod.* If you're having a problem (the line at your feet on the cast, the line hitting you, snapped flies, the line and leader bunching up in front of you, etc.), look at what the tip of your rod is doing.

Except when you want the line to drift down in front of you, *your rod tip will not be lower than eleven o'clock or one o'clock.*

Don't cast haphazardly. *Aim where you want the cast to go.* This is a good habit to get into. Many neophyte casters are so caught up in the rudiments of casting that they forget the purpose of the cast is to get the fly where you want it.

At all times *strive for a fluid, smooth motion— and a quick wrist* (we'll explain *quick wrist* in a moment).

This isn't volleyball. *Don't muscle the rod!* Besides the fact that it will wear you out after a

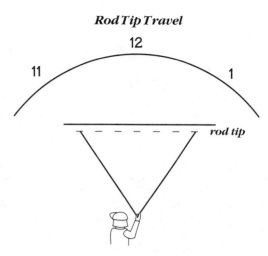

The rod must travel in a straight line.

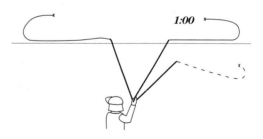

If you drop the rod below the one o'clock position, it throws off the rhythm of your cast, and you usually will lose control.

Casting is a fluid, flowing motion. It's a rhythm.

Practice in your front yard or the nearest park or school—anywhere you can lay the line out and provide a soft place for your fly to land.

couple of hours on the water, it's not good technique, and you won't cast effectively. The rod should be doing nearly all the work, not you. Your job is to guide and control the rod.

Where to Practice

You can't cast in your living room. You need some space. At the least, you'll need about 60 feet to practice—30 feet in front of you and 30 feet in back. Before long, you'll need more room than this.

A nice front lawn is a good place to start. If this isn't convenient, your local park will do just fine. You want to cast over grass, since grass isn't hard on your line like dirt, pavement, concrete, and rocks. We have heard of casters so eager to learn that they used the road as a practice zone. Besides wearing out a good fly line in record time, they had to dodge cars and trucks at the last moment. We appreciate their enthusiasm, but not their lack of good sense.

Once you get to where you are going to practice, lay your rod down and pull off 20 feet of fly line. This will be enough for you to work with for the time being. Many fish are caught with this much line or less.

You should have about 8 feet of leader attached to the end of the fly line. At this point, don't worry about the leader being tapered. A strip of old monofilament off your spinning rod will do. To the end of your leader attach a small piece of bright yarn (so you can see where your fly would be going).

The Back Cast

Now we are going to have you practice bringing the line up off the grass (water) in front of you and going into the back cast. We won't worry about the front cast yet. (Casting will be easier to do on the water since the water puts more friction on the line.) Practice the following steps until you feel comfortable:

1. Grip the rod (your thumb forward, pointing toward the direction of the rod).

2. Tuck the line under the index finger of the hand gripping the rod. This is an important habit to get into when you fish and when you cast.

3. Lift the line up smoothly until the rod tip reaches the ten o'clock position.

4. Bring your arm back smoothly but briskly, accelerating until your rod gets to the one o'clock position. The fly line will follow your rod tip.

5. Stop.

6. Let the line fall in back of you. The line should lie out flat in back of you before it falls down.

Then reverse the process: Turn around and cast the line in the other direction. (At first you may have to lay down your rod and straighten the line.)

Practice these steps ten or twenty times until the line lies flat in back of you before it drops.

To tighten your loop, which is the shape of your line during the cast, speed up your wrist even more

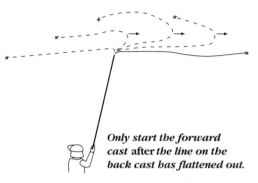

The Effective Back Cast (Making sure the line flattens out)

Only start the forward cast after the line on the *back cast has flattened out.*

Because you are looking over your shoulder, you can see when the line flattens out. If you cast while the line is still arched (or candy-caned), it will snap, possibly whip off the fly, and ruin the forward cast as well as your accuracy. If you start the forward cast too soon, line will pile up at your feet.

The Tight Loop

The Wide Loop

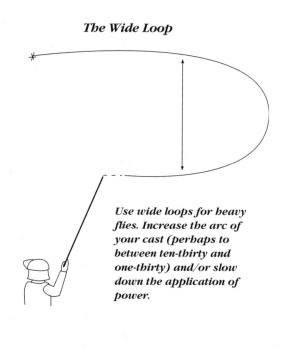

Use wide loops for heavy flies. Increase the arc of your cast (perhaps to between ten-thirty and one-thirty) and/or slow down the application of power.

A tight loop allows you a longer cast. The tight loop is the darling of the dry fly caster. To get a narrow, tighter loop, close up the arc by limiting your range of motion to between eleven-thirty and twelve-thirty. You can also speed up the acceleration in the application of power.

Line Loops

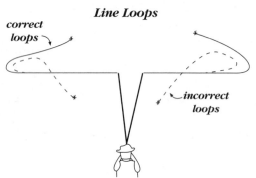

correct loops

incorrect loops

Your loops should look like books. They shouldn't sag. If they sag, you'll get windknots, and your cast will be hampered.

during the last part of the cast. A *quick wrist* means to move your wrist more rapidly than normal casting acceleration. The sharper the thrust, the tighter the loop. On the back cast, put this added speed from twelve-thirty to one o'clock. (On the front cast, you'll thrust from eleven-thirty to one o'clock.)

The Front Cast

Again, strip off 20 feet of fly line. This time the line should be in back of you. This exercise is a little more contrived than the back cast since you'd likely never start with the line in back of you. Still, we think it's a very useful exercise. It will be important to place the line quite straight on the ground so it will pick up easier.

1. Grip the rod the way we showed you.
2. Tuck the line under your index finger.
3. Lift the line up smoothly until the rod tip is near two o'clock.

The Front Cast

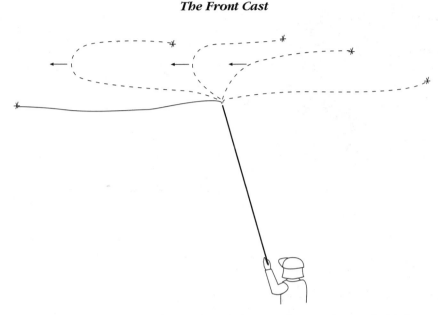

Wait for your line to lie out in front of you before you start to execute the back cast. This is much easier to do than back casting because you don't have to worry about looking over your shoulder.

4. Bring your arm forward smoothly but briskly, accelerating until your rod gets to the eleven o'clock position. The fly line will follow your rod tip.

5. Stop.

6. Let the line fall in front of you. The line should lie out flat in front of you before it falls down.

Then reverse the process: Turn around and cast the line in the other direction. (At first you may have to lay down your rod and straighten the line.)

Practice these steps ten or twenty times until the line lies flat in front of you before it drops.

Don't move on until you feel you have the back cast and the front cast under control. Practice casting a few more times if need be. A good way to tell if you are ready is by looking at your line. If the line is lying out fairly flat before it drops on the front and the back casts, it's time to move on.

Hold the line with your index finger and pull in the excess (or strip out) with the opposite hand.

See how the line is lying out flat? Don't start your forward cast until your back cast has flattened out.

Learning these two steps will help you put the process of casting together. Several things should have happened. First, you noticed that the tip of the rod did all the work and controlled the line. Second, you felt the line on the rod. Now let's put the two movements together.

Combining the Front and Back Casts

Instead of letting the line drop, we are now going to put the two casts together. Again, strip off 20 feet of line. The line should be in front of you.

When you are fishing, you will often directly face the area you are casting to. For the time being, however, stand at a forty-five-degree angle when you cast so you can keep an eye on that back cast.

Generally, if there is a problem, it's with the back cast, since it's the one we don't see as easily. Also, a good back cast sets up what we are going to do on the front cast. If the back cast is weak, the rest of the cast will be ineffective also.

The way to speed up your learning curve is to constantly keep an eye on your line. That's why we want you to stand at an angle. First, face your target area directly. Then turn forty-five degrees to your right if you are right-handed. (Lefties go the other way.) This allows you to keep an eye over your shoulder and on how the line is lying out.

You will notice that steps 1 through 4 are identical to the first four steps of the front cast that you've already practiced.

1. Grip the rod the way we showed you.
2. Tuck the line under your index finger.
3. Lift the line up smoothly until you get to the ten o'clock position.
4. Bring your arm back evenly but briskly, accelerating until your rod gets to the one o'clock position. The fly line will follow your rod tip.
5. Pause for an instant as the line flattens out in back of you. When the line flattens out, it will be parallel to the ground. You can see this easily since you are at an angle to the target area.

6. When the line is flat, smoothly make the forward cast—powering forward, keeping in mind that you are working within the eleven o'clock and one o'clock positions. Keep the tip of your rod straight. This will keep the line under control.

7. At eleven o'clock, stop the rod tip and let the line flatten out in front of you.

8. Immediately repeat the back cast.

The front and back casts together are an orchestrated motion. Don't forget to pause and let the line flatten out before executing the cast.

Knowing this striper's comfort zone allowed Dave to quickly home in on where the school of striper was holding. Accurate casting helped him catch dozens of fish in one afternoon.

Aiming

It really helps if you can hit what you are aiming at. Often when you fish, you'll find the angler who can cast and hit his or her target is the angler who catches fish. After you have the cast under control, try aiming at a specific target: a shoe box, a hat, a Frisbee—anything you can see.

Lay the rod on the ground and stretch out the line and leader. You should have about 20 feet of fly line out. Set your target a foot or two back from the piece of yarn at the end of the leader. If you feel ambitious, set several targets out.

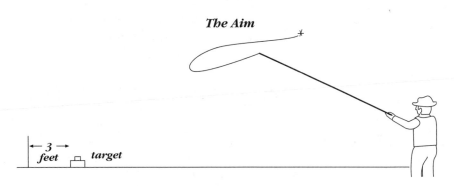

When you start to practice, aim about 3 feet beyond the target.

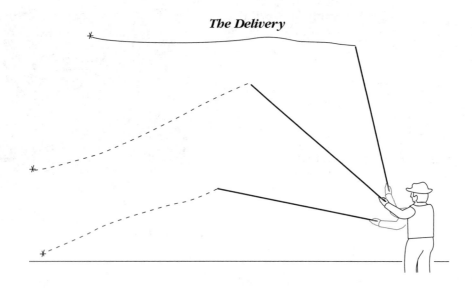

The Delivery

Once the line has flattened out, gently drop the rod tip to the nine o'clock position.

Pick up your rod and make several casts.

1. Keep your eye on the target.

2. When your rod tip gets to eleven o'clock, pause slightly.

3. Drop your arm as you let the line drift down.

4. Keep the tip of your rod pointed above the target.

Practice at several targets to the right and left of center. Work on letting your fly line drift down. Your leader with the yarn tied on the end should fall near the target.

If your line is falling in a large gob in front of you or the line and leader are falling in a clump and not lying out flat, watch your rod tip. There's a good chance you are dropping your arm so your rod tip isn't traveling in a straight line between the one o'clock and eleven o'clock positions. Since your line follows the rod, the line likewise is not straight.

Look at your back cast. Is the line lying out straight?

If you're having problems, practice the front and back casts separately a few times. Sometimes when you put the casts together, it takes a little rehearsing to get the motions fluid.

Adding Line to Your Cast

You can't cast forever with 20 feet of fly line. You'll need to add some distance to your cast. You do this by feeding out line. Don't try adding line, however, until you have the other steps under control.

Start by stripping off 20 feet of fly line. Do front and back casts just to work on your timing for a few minutes. Now let the line drift in front of you.

Adding Line: The Back Cast

1. Grip the rod.
2. Don't forget to hold the line under your index finger. You have to have a tight hold on your line to effectively cast. This is called *controlling the line*.
3. With your left hand (if you are a right-hander), strip off about 7 additional feet of line. The 7 feet of stripped line should be hanging *behind* your finger and the reel. Let this line drop at your feet.
4. Lift the rod and line up smoothly until the rod tip is at the ten o'clock position.
5. Bring your arm back smoothly but briskly, accelerating until your rod gets to the one o'clock position. The fly line will follow your rod tip.
6. As the line is *unrolling* backward, release your index finger and let the 7 feet of slack line "shoot" backward as it is pulled by the power of the retreating line.
7. Let the line fall in back of you.

Then reverse the process: Turn around and cast the line in the other direction, following these same seven steps. (If necessary, first lay down your rod and straighten the line in back of you.)

Practice this feeding cast until the line lies back smoothly. Work until the line is fed out crisply.

This beginning caster is getting the hang of casting and making excellent progress. Observe how the line is curved—he's not bringing the rod tip back in a straight line. You can be successful the first time you hit the water—even if you've never picked up a fly rod.

In some waters it might be necessary to kneel so the fish won't see your shadow. Notice how straight the line is on the forward cast.

A proper cast and a proper drift are essential to success. It takes practice. Jon-Michael, Michael's son, was casting and catching fish when he was nine. He started practicing in the front yard.

When the line is lying flat before falling nicely behind you, it's time to work on the forward cast.

Adding Line: The Front Cast

1. Grip the rod.

2. Don't forget to hold the line under your index finger. You have to have a tight hold on your line to effectively cast. This is called *controlling the line*.

3. With your left hand, strip off about 7 additional feet of line. (The 7 feet of stripped line should be hanging *behind* your finger and the reel.) Let this line drop at your feet.

4. Lift the rod and line up smoothly until the rod tip is near the two o'clock position.

5. Bring your arm forward smoothly but briskly, accelerating until your rod gets to the eleven o'clock position. The fly line will follow your rod tip.

6. As the line is *unrolling* forward, release your index finger and let the 7 feet of slack line "shoot" forward as it's pulled by the power of the advancing line.

7. Let the line fall in front of you.

Then reverse the process: Turn around and cast the line in the other direction, following these same seven steps. (If necessary, first lay down your rod and straighten the line in back of you.)

Practice this feeding cast ten or twenty times until the line lies flat in front of you before it drops.

Adding Line: Combining the Back and Front Casts

Since you have already put the back and forward casts together, we won't detail the procedure again here. Practice adding line to your cast and hitting a target. If you need to false-cast several times to get ready, do it. Then let the line drift down.

Now that you have learned how to add 7 feet of line to the front or back casts, how do you add line on both casts consecutively?

When you are actually casting, you'll sometimes have to strip out line during the casting movement.

(You certainly don't want to stop the process in order to pull off more line.) There's an easy technique: Start by stripping out some extra line before you cast. Strip off about 10 to 14 feet, and simply release half on the back cast and the other half on the forward cast. With one complete casting motion (backward and forward), you have added 10 to 14 feet to your cast.

Once you've fed this stripped-out line into your cast, however, you may want to feed out even more line. Here's how you do it:

While your rod is coming forward, simply strip more line off the reel with your left hand. Then as the rod reaches eleven o'clock and is starting to advance, release your index finger, and the power of the advancing line will pull this excess out.

When you are stripping and adding line during the cast, work with short amounts until you have the action down. Practice what you have learned until the motion is smooth and graceful. After you have mastered adding line on the back and forward casts consecutively, you can work on getting even more line out.

Also work on line speed. The faster the line moves, the longer you can cast. Work with your wrist snaps and keeping a tight loop. To gain more speed you can use a *haul*—which means pulling down on the line with your left hand as you are moving your rod from the eleven o'clock to one o'clock positions (or vice versa). Doing this increases the tension on the line, and it travels faster. It's like supercharging your line.

Always aim for a target.

Accuracy is more important than distance.

Here's Dave fishing on his lunch hour—nothing unusual.

Roll Casting: Your Best Line Forward

While the back cast is a cast you'll do often, there are fishing situations when it's the wrong thing to do. During these times, it is good to know how to do the roll cast.

The Roll Cast

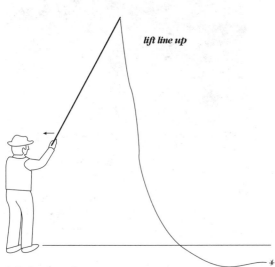

lift line up

1. Raise the rod up.

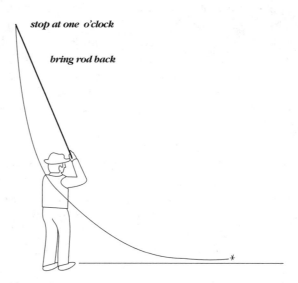

stop at one o'clock

bring rod back

2. Raise backward until line drifts behind the elbow.

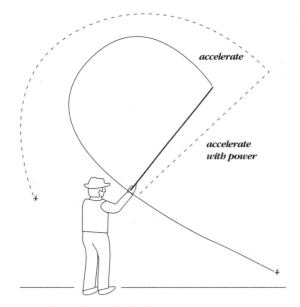

accelerate

accelerate with power

3. Accelerate forward with full power.

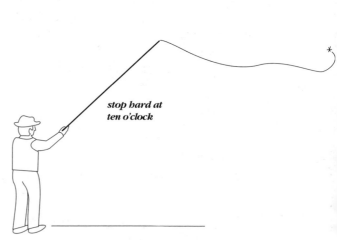

stop hard at ten o'clock

4. Stop. Line rolls to strike zone.

Compared to the basic cast, the roll cast is easy and can be mastered quickly. As the name implies, to do this cast you will "roll" the line out. You start your line moving in a rolling motion. The power of the motion picks up the line still in the water and flips it where you aim. You don't lift your line completely out of the water as you normally would with the basic cast. Instead, you pull a little slack into your line and flip it in the direction you desire.

There are several benefits in knowing how to do a roll cast. Perhaps the most important one is that it keeps your line in the water longer so you have a better chance of catching a fish. Instead of going through the motions of a basic cast, you simply flip your line to where you want to reposition it in one elementary movement. This is especially handy when you are trying to drift over a certain location. Once the drift has gone over the likely strike zone, you reposition the fly and line for another quick drift. This way you aren't wasting time casting or going through the full drift. Instead you are covering the best area again and again. Over a fifteen-minute period, you could get a dozen or more extra drifts— and this translates into more fish.

When you are fishing a wet fly, which is usually heavier, this cast is even easier. An additional advantage is that it doesn't matter if you slap the surface water with your line, which you sometimes do with this cast. Often, casting a heavy, wet fly can be a little complicated. The roll cast takes some of the headache out of the job.

To effectively do the roll cast, you really need to have your line on the water. The water friction on the line helps you perform this cast in a crisp, effective manner. It loads the rod. We suggest you practice it on a lawn until you get the movement right. The execution of the line will not be as crisp as you'd like, though, because the line is not on water. In fact, the line may bunch up a little. This is to be expected.

What we want you to do is get the motion down. Then when you are on the water, you will be

If you can do a roll cast, you can catch fish. Jon-Michael is at the beginning stages of his roll cast. This cast is a good way to keep your fly in the water longer, which means you'll have a better chance to get a hook up.

Even experts like our friend Lee utilize the roll cast. This cast is especially useful for wet-fly casting when you don't need a delicate presentation.

roll casting like a champ. After a few casts you'll feel like an expert.

How to Do the Roll Cast

Remember, it's the water drag that loads the rod. (The lawn isn't even a good second, but it's all we have to practice on.) Nevertheless, begin by stripping off about 20 feet of fly line. Then just carry out the following simple steps:

1. Slowly lift the rod to the one o'clock position. The line will drape in front of you as you lift the rod, dragging the line across the lawn (water). As you reach the one o'clock position, the line from the tip of the rod will be hanging a little behind you.

2. Sharply, but smoothly, accelerate the rod to the ten o'clock position, pointing the rod tip to where you want your fly to go.

Some people find that bending at the waist as they put power into the forward cast helps the line roll out easier. We're not really sure why this works, but it does.

Adding Line to the Roll Cast

Sometimes you'll want to add some line to your roll cast.

To do this, merely strip line off the reel in the same manner as you would for the basic cast. As the line is accelerating forward in the roll motion, release your index finger (the finger holding the line against the rod handle). The force of the line will pull the line you've stripped out and give you additional length.

Many successful wet fly casters use a roll cast 70 percent of the time. As an added note, a few years ago we went to a favorite series of ponds Dave likes to fish in the winter. Dave used the roll cast most of the time to reposition his fly. A gentleman, somewhat frustrated, commented to Michael that Dave had *really* out-fished him. The man had been using the same basic rod and fly line as Dave (an olive leech and #5-weight line). He'd done okay, but since it was a cold, brisk January day with a stout wind, he had to really work to get his casts positioned. Dave didn't.

After Dave had worked the water he thought was productive, he simply rolled his cast back into the good water and started the process again. Dave caught three times as many fish as this fellow, but it only stands to reason; he had his fly in the water three times as long.

Serpentine Cast: Cut Yourself Some Slack

We haven't talked about mending yet. Rest assured, we will later in more detail. For now, *mending* means adjusting your line so you get a natural drift. There are a number of ways to mend a line. However, there is one mending cast we'd like to introduce: the serpentine cast.

This is an excellent cast you can implement to put slack into your line as you cast. This is very helpful when you are fishing in waters with varying currents. The advantage of a serpentine cast is that your line adjusts (mends) without moving the fly.

The idea is to throw a series of S's in your line as it lies on the water in front of you. The slack in the line keeps your fly drifting naturally, so there's no drag. It takes a while for the current to take the S's out of your line before the drag starts.

How to Do the Serpentine Cast

This is an easy cast to make. You can practice it on the lawn and master it quickly. This cast is a variation of the basic cast.

1. Make a standard cast. (Do a front and back cast to warm up.)

2. Make the forward delivery cast and let the line flatten out.

3. With the line flattening, shake the rod gently

The Serpentine Cast

Shake your rod tip before the line hits the water.

No matter how careful you are, you're going to get hung up. Here, Dave hooked a very fine branch on the Green River.

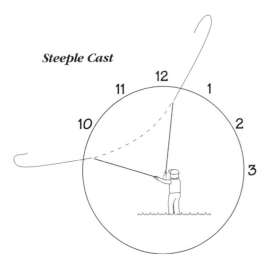

Steeple Cast

To prevent your back cast from snagging, stop at twelve o'clock so the line goes straight up.

back and forth as the line is drifting down. The more shakes you put in the rod tip, the more S's you'll get in your line.

The fly will fall about where you aimed—perhaps a few feet short. As you practice, you will get the hang of this S cast. Everyone shakes a little differently. Learn what it takes for you to cast a tight S and a loose S pattern.

Steeple Cast: Highly Effective

What happens if you can't do a back cast?

Sometimes the best places to fish are the worst places to cast. Perhaps you have your back to a steep bank. Maybe there's a wall of brush or trees. Knowing how to perform a good steeple cast will be a real bonus. You will be able to dry your fly, or more important, you will be able to do this style of back cast.

You won't be able to get as much distance out of a steeple cast as you would from a back cast, but with practice you can get 30 to 50 feet.

How to Do the Steeple Cast

The forward part of the cast is just like the forward part of the basic cast. What's different is how you execute the back cast. Instead of coming back as you normally would, your back cast will go almost straight up—shaped, as you have guessed, like the side of a steeple.

You'll want to start with 15 or 20 feet of fly line. With a small amount of line, this cast isn't difficult to perform. As you work with more line, it becomes a little more complicated.

With this cast you will be working between the ten o'clock and twelve o'clock positions.

1. Start with the basic cast, except bring the forward cast down to ten o'clock (instead of eleven o'clock) and let the line flatten out. (Hint: Make sure you are angled forty-five degrees so that you are

able to look over your shoulder to keep track of the line.)

2. Bring the rod back as you would in a back cast. But at twelve o'clock, stop the rod in a more exaggerated manner.

3. As you are stopping at twelve o'clock, lift your hand up about a foot and make an inside arc with the tip of the rod. (Remember, the line will do what the rod tip tells it to.)

If you have done the cast correctly, the line will form a steep arc into the air—sloping at the bottom but shooting almost straight up, like a steeple. This cast takes a little practice. If you are having trouble, try shortening the line.

This is a cast you'll want to practice under practice conditions—either on the lawn or at your favorite fishing place. Don't practice this cast under steeple-casting conditions, or you'll be picking your line out of the trees.

Some casters get this cast fast; others have to work at it a little more. For example, Michael has never really perfected it.

Reach Cast: Adjusting to Current Trends

The reach cast is another mending cast. It's used to put a mend in your line before it touches the water. After you have looked at the current and seen how you need to adjust your line, cast so the body of the line is either upstream or downstream of the area you want your fly to drift through.

Because the water flow isn't even and the body of the line and the fly and leader often float at different speeds, drag is created. Few self-respecting fish will look at a fly with drag. This cast evens things up. The current moves the slack in the line before it can pull the fly.

After you get the hang of the reach cast, we think you'll find it one of the most valuable fly fishing tools. Because you have a good working knowledge of the basic cast, this line will be easy to

When you fish with children, it's important to teach them how to cast to places where fish are holding. They will be more successful, and you'll have a fishing partner for life.

Sometimes it's necessary to mend your line during the cast—like this reach cast.

master. While the serpentine cast is useful, this cast will give you more control overall.

How to Do the Reach Cast

Start your practice with about 20 to 30 feet of line—whatever feels comfortable. You start with the basic cast and modify it on the forward movement. You'll want to practice the reach cast to the left and right.

With the reach cast, your fly will be on target while the body of the fly line will be right or left of the fly. To do the reach cast, wait until your line is starting to straighten out during your forward cast. Then simply reach with the rod a short distance to either the left or the right.

Try it a variety of ways and make note of the differences. As your forward cast is starting to straighten out, reach with the rod to the left about 18 inches. Now do the same thing, but this time reach to the left about 6 inches. You should notice a difference.

Now let's try it to the right. As your forward cast is starting to straighten out, reach with the rod to the right about 18 inches. Now do the same thing, but this time reach to the right about 6 inches. You should notice a difference.

Every fishing condition is different. How much reach you need will vary with the cast and water conditions.

For further practice, set up a target on the lawn at 35 feet. Come back about 10 feet and set another target 5 feet to the right and one 5 feet to the left. Practice so your fly hits the target but the body of the line lands on the left side of the left target or the right side of the right target. Then move the side targets closer together and practice with more distance between you and the targets.

4

SEEING PAST THE SURFACE

Judging the Water

Do you have to look at life like a fish?

Not necessarily. A fish has a pretty narrow view of the world. You do, however, have to know about fish and understand something about how a fish lives. Remember the old adage: *Twelve percent of the people fishing catch 88 percent of the fish.*

Luck has little to do with catching fish day in and day out.

Why? Successful fly casters don't necessarily think like fish. But they do know fish behavior. They understand many of the important things you need to know to catch fish consistently. They have learned what fish eat, what feeding patterns fish have, what a fish's comfort and safety needs are, and where fish are in a stream or lake.

The 12 percent who catch most of the fish do it consistently, in almost any water, at almost any time. They catch fish because they understand how fish act and react. More important, they understand what fish need.

Fish don't really think. They simply react to surroundings. We want you to understand what makes a fish tick, understand what makes it react. Let's take a look at fish behavior.

Learn to read the water so you can catch fish. If you know where the fish are, you can cast to them. Many casters don't spend enough time learning about fish and the fish's world. See past the surface and learn the best places to drift your fly.

When you look at a stretch of water like this, what do you see? Where will you find fish, the biggest fish?

Fish Are Only Human: The Search for Food

The first thing we need to know is that fish are either *active* or *dormant*. An active fish is a fish that's feeding or looking for food. A dormant fish is one that's resting, a fish that is not actively feeding at the moment.

An active fish is easier to catch since it's on the prowl and will go wherever the food is—even into uncomfortable or unsafe water. A dormant fish can be caught—it's still opportunistic about food—but it won't go out of its way to investigate, and it will stay only in water that is very comfortable.

You will run across the word *lie* in this book and in other fishing literature or conversations. It's a term for a place that a fish holds. It simply means where the fish lies, holds, hides, or waits. It can refer to where the fish is resting when it's dormant or where the fish is waiting in the stream for the current to bring its food.

A lie is where the fish holds in the water for one reason or another. If it's not for feeding, a lie is a place where all or most of a fish's needs are met— food, comfort, shelter.

To understand fish further, let's look at the single driving force in a fish's life: the search for food. The first part of learning how to read or judge the water is knowing how to judge fish. Since feeding is central to a fish's life, knowing about its food cycle is the first major step in judging fish.

A caster who just wades into the water and throws flies is a caster who isn't going to catch too many fish. The caster who makes a concerted effort to judge the water, and fishes according to what has been learned, is the one who will be reeling in fish. When you first look at the water, you'll be looking for several things:

- Where a fish is feeding
- What a fish is feeding upon
- Where a fish is resting

You'll also be looking to find out:

- Where a fish *might* be feeding
- What a fish *might* be feeding upon
- Where a fish *might* be resting

In a stream or a river, the food comes to the fish via the conveyer belt known as the current or drift. When a fish is hungry, it goes to the most likely spot in the stream and *waits* for the conveyer belt to bring its dinner. As a result, a stream fish often has to make snap decisions about its food—if it doesn't, the food is gone.

In a lake or a pond, a fish must go more directly to the food. It is more likely to *patrol* or cruise to fulfill its food needs. This fish has a chance to study its food more carefully.

Lakes pose a special challenge. Where do you start? Look for structure and go from there. This point is an excellent place to begin casting.

These are the main differences between fish feeding habits in these two types of waters. At times you will have to fish a stream differently from the way you fish a lake. The basic needs of the fish are the same, but how those needs are met is different. Once you understand, you will begin catching more fish.

The Nature of Feeding Fish

If you were a fish, where would be the best place to get your food delivered to you? It's easy to see why those fly casters who know where a fish is likely to lie will catch more fish. Casting so your fly drifts through good lies, especially feeding lies, greatly increases your chances of hooking a hungry fish. It's also easy to see why the person who casts to an unlikely spot can be there all day without so much as a bite.

When a fish is feeding, it will lie where it can get the most food with the least amount of effort. Fish, after all, are only human. *Fish are lazy!* They won't work any more than they have to. The more food a fish can consume with the least amount of energy expended, the better. Big fish are those that learn how to make every bite count. A fish that survives

It's necessary to study the water so you spend your time fishing where the fish are. A good pair of polarized glasses is a must—it will help you see past the glare into the water.

To hold a fish like this, you'll need to understand its needs—specifically where and how it eats.

learns to position itself in a current and move just a few inches to eat bugs floating on the water.

It's a case of *energy gained feeding vs. energy lost collecting.* Calories taken in must exceed calories expended.

What Will a Fish Eat?

Anything it can! One particular insect. Or nothing at all.

There are times when people eat everything in sight. Everything looks good, and we don't seem to get full. We don't discriminate since it all looks tasty. At other times we are interested only in one or two things. That's all we want. We want lots of one thing, and nothing else will do. Then there are times when we aren't hungry. We might take a little nibble of something out of conditioned response, but food is the last thing on our minds.

Fish are the same way.

Sometimes fish are very opportunistic eaters. They'll eat anything in sight. This is an angler's favorite time to fish since it's hard to do anything wrong. The fish are very active and seem to be very hungry. Any attractor pattern, anything that looks like fish food, will hammer a fish—even a dry fly fished wet. At times like this, about any fly in your box will work. The fish have a mighty hunger, and they're out to feast and gorge.

At other times, fish are hungry but are systematic about eating. They are focused on one or two insects, and if you want any fishing action, you'd better *match the hatch* exactly. If you throw out a fly, it had better be a fly that looks just like what they are eating—the same size and color, acting or floating the way the natural counterpart does. For a fish, even a small hatch of bugs is worth feeding on if the fish can eat in volume and do so without expending too much energy. When a fish is focused on one particular hatch, you should be, too. We'll talk more about the various hatches in the next chapter so that you can identify them and know how to fish a fly to fool a clever trout.

Sometimes the fish don't seem to be interested in feeding at all. They're dormant for one reason or another. At times like this, you can still catch fish by throwing a fly that looks tempting and is presented perfectly. Fish take such a fly more out of a conditioned response than hunger. This is your best chance of hooking up with a good fish. On the bright side, such a dormant mood rarely lasts long, and you can outwait the moody fish. Hunger will set in, or other conditions will change. Sometimes moving to a new section of water is all you need to do.

Even if all the fish seem to be shut down at once, it's still worth fishing. Michael calls this *the trout pout*—all the fish seem to be pouting at once, and no one wants to come out and play. Keep fishing, however, since there's always a trout out there that can be had. Fishing runs in cycles and is hot and cold accordingly.

Food, Top and Bottom: The Bugs

"Top" is the surface, the film, the place you fish a dry fly. "Bottom" is under the surface, often near the bottom but anywhere under the film, the place you fish a wet fly.

It is important to try and determine which bug or bugs are the most active at the time you are fishing. Which is the easiest and biggest meal? Once you make this determination, you have a much better idea of which fly you should select from your box. (We will get into a more serious study of bugs, *entomology,* later.)

Although it's important to identify which bug or bugs are the most prevalent, sometimes this is easier said than done. Bugs are small, and there may be several types flitting about, so it can be hard to identify the right ones.

There are several things you can do. You can get lucky and catch a fish, pump its stomach with a

Every time you arrive at a new part of the stream you must ask yourself, "Where would I hide if I were a fish?"

The anglers in this shot aren't where they are by accident. The caster in the foreground is working the water around a large boulder—a likely place for fish to escape the current and wait for food.

stomach pump, and see which bugs it has been eating. Or you can bug-net the water, thus capturing the most common bugs. Or you can watch the fish and see which bugs they seem to be taking.

Sometimes this bug identification is frustrating because it delays your fishing. But a few moments spent at this task will help determine your fishing strategy, and fly fishing without a clear idea of what the fish are taking is like going on a vacation without a road map.

Where a Fish Will Lie to Get Food "Delivered"

Dave always tells his clients, "Be thinking, where is the fish food?" This is very good advice.

It stands to reason that some parts of the water are better than others from a hungry fish's point of view. What is it about some sections of stream that make good feeding lies?

First, there has to be a food supply. But there has to be more than that. The supply has to be accessible and as easy as possible to get. To facilitate this, the water needs to be slow or it needs to be broken up.

Depending on the strength of the current, it takes a certain amount of energy for a fish to hold in the drift. Rather than stay in the swift water and burn up a lot of energy, a fish will seek out an obstacle that breaks the flow. This is the first element of a good lie. Look at the stream and try to determine where the current is broken up or slowed down. Fish will lie here because there is protection from the current and a way for them to save valuable calories. Another consideration for the fish is that a break in the current slows the conveyer-belt current down, and the fish has a better chance to look over its food.

A good fly caster looks over the water before starting to fish. Besides looking for food sources, the caster looks for places where the flow is broken—what are called *seams* in the flow of the stream.

A seam is any break or disruption in the flow of the stream—any place where the current is altered or modified in any way.

Look for the obvious seams first: rocks, boulders, logs, a shelf, old cars, a sandbar, any blockage of the current. Some folks refer to these seam-creating objects as *structure.*

Next, look for swirls on the surface that might indicate large rocks on the bottom that could break up the course. Also look for areas where two different currents meet or places where there is a moss line or a feeder creek.

Look for Places That Might Produce Fish Food

Besides waiting for food to be brought down by the current, even lazy stream and river trout will go and do a little hunting. If there is no apparent activity, there are places you can focus on.

Sandy bottoms are great places to swim, but they usually don't produce much food. Casting over a sandy bottom, unless you have reason to believe that food is there, wouldn't be a good way to spend your time.

Casting near a moss line, on the other hand, is a good place to start. A lot of organisms that fish call food live in this watery jungle. Bugs and small fish live and hide in the moss, and fish know it. It's a good place to prowl if you are a hungry fish.

It's not unusual to see lurking fish all of a sudden plow into weeds or moss to dislodge bugs and other edible matter. Occasionally you'll even see a fish grab a big glob of moss with its mouth and shake bugs off the vegetation. The fish will then drop back and intercept what falls off. Moss lines are made for good fishing.

The Opportunists

In spite of all that's said and done, fish are opportunistic.

It's important to have a good selection of flies so you can match the food that the fish are eating.

Know where a fish lies in the water—where does it feed, where does it rest, what part of the stream does it like to stay in?

If it looks like they can get a tender morsel and not expend too much energy getting it, they will. You can use this to your advantage. If you are fishing a midge hatch (a very small fly, #20 or smaller) and are not doing well because you can't match up the hatch exactly, you might prey upon a fish's sense of opportunism. The fish are feeding very selectively, and you have nothing that can match it. However, you might tie on an ant or a hopper—a fly that is considerably larger. Occasionally you can get even a selective fish to rise for your presentation.

Why?

Because a fish is opportunistic and somehow knows that for the same movement it can get a hopper or an ant that is a dozen times larger than what it is eating—more calories for the same amount of work. (The fact that these terrestrials are very tasty doesn't hurt, either.)

Shelter and Safety: Covering Their Tails

If food is the primary concern for a fish, shelter and safety are close seconds.

Predators In and Out of the Water

Fish aren't high on the food chain.

Fish are usually quite spooky, and rightly so. For most of their lives, something is after their respective tails. And if a fish is going to learn how to survive, it has to learn how to protect itself. If it's not snakes, otters, minks, and birds of prey, it's raccoons, bears, and anglers. And don't forget the biggest predator of all, larger fish. A fish is always looking over its shoulder. It faces danger from above and below. Of the few fish that make it to the fry stage, even fewer make it to 12 inches. And fewer still grow larger.

Fish get cocky if they survive. Then they feel it's their right to eat any fish that's just a few inches shorter. Being a fish is a giant game of King of the Hill. As you survive, you move up to the next best place, knocking the other guy out of the way if you're bigger. Being the biggest fish gives you the right to hold in the best lies, and so you get fatter. A big fish is hardest to catch because it has seen more and has lived a longer, more paranoid life. As a result of making it up the ladder of survival, it doesn't have to be so aggressive any longer. Once a fish gets big, its life is a lot easier.

Ever wonder why you catch so many small fish? Small fish, because they have to survive, are by nature more aggressive and thus easier to catch. They have to stay in less desirable water and work harder for their food.

Current

For fish, seams in the current are not only good places to feed but are also good places for shelter because the fish don't have to fight the main current. A productive seam for both fish and fly caster is where fast and slow currents meet.

Here a fish can rest on one side in the slow current and observe the food going by in the faster lane. If a fish is positioned correctly, all that is required for eating is to move its hungry head and feast from items on the tasty buffet.

Light

A fish is most visible and vulnerable in the direct light, and this makes it uncomfortable and nervous. In this situation, you'll notice that fish are skittish—especially if the water is shallow. As the water gets deeper, they get less panicky.

Always look for a more comfortable fish in the shadows. Look for shadows on the water. Is there a shadowy side of a boulder or a rock? Is there an undercut bank that offers shade? Is there an overhanging tree or shadow from a steep bank? Look closely. Can you spot movement? Fish love to hang out in the shadows.

Knowing how a fish lives and what it wants will help you present your fly successfully. In this photo, our friend Lee shows off a fine brown before releasing it. Lee hooked this fish at dawn, when the light was low.

This water is a lot deeper than it looks. Where in this pool would a fish's needs be met?

This doesn't mean that fish won't go into direct sunlight. They just don't like it. If you are fishing, you'll have to be very careful. Make sure you don't throw a shadow or let fish see your movement. The direct sun makes you more visible, as well. As you've probably guessed, direct sun is known for making bugs active and for hatches. If it's worth it, a fish will venture out into the light and eat. But the feeding will be fast and furious and nervous. After the last bite, the fish will swiftly dart back to a safer place.

Depth

Depth is a comfort to a fish. It masks the effects of direct light, and it's a buffer from surface predators. It's a security blanket. For the fish, from the time it was young, depth meant safety. When a fish gets spooked, it goes deep.

If there is no structure in the water—no rocks, logs, or other shelter—the depth of the water is a "structure" of sorts that offers the fish a semblance of sanctuary.

Comfort Zones

A fish needs a cozy temperature zone, just as we do. If a person gets too cold, he or she will put on clothes. If it gets too hot, some of the clothes get taken off. A fish can't take off or add on clothes. The only way this cold-blooded creature can get comfortable is by finding comfortable water. Let's consider two important factors: temperature and oxygen.

Temperature

To help make an *ideal* lie, consider what we've talked about thus far and add *temperature*. Being cold-blooded, different fish have different temperature zones they feel comfortable in. When fish are dormant, they will seek a part of the stream or lake that has shelter and the right temperature.

As the seasons change and water levels fluctuate, a fish's ideal lie will change to meet the conditions. That means a section of the stream that might be an ideal lie in the summer might not be an ideal lie during the winter or fall. As the temperature of the water changes, so does the fish's lie. Unless the water temperature remains constant (a river or stream coming from a dam or a spring creek), the fish will change its home.

The effective fly caster knows a fish will seek water as close to its ideal comfort zone as it can. This is especially true when it's dormant. When trout are active and feeding, they don't always have this luxury. Sometimes a fish needs to feed in uncomfortable water. The more uncomfortable it is, the quicker the fish will get in to feed and get back to more friendly water. A fish likes its comfort.

Following are the approximate ideal water-temperature ranges for four kinds of trout:

- Brook Trout: 48 to 65 degrees Fahrenheit
- Cutthroat Trout: 52 to 65 degrees Fahrenheit
- Rainbow Trout: 52 to 65 degrees Fahrenheit
- Brown Trout: 52 to 68 degrees Fahrenheit
- Largemouth Bass: 73 to 78 degrees Fahrenheit

Many anglers carry a small pocket thermometer to check the water temperature. This is very useful to a stream or river angler—and it is critical to a pond or a lake angler in order to know how deep to fish.

Fish are most active in the middle of their ideal temperature range.

The middle of the range usually means good fishing. When a fish is comfortable, it will go on long feeding binges. It will be more aggressive. As you get to either extreme of the ideal range—or outside the range—a fish will become more sluggish and less likely to look at a fly unless it floats right past its nose.

Oxygen

Oxygen is the lifeblood of the water ecosystem.

Fish breathe by processing oxygen from the

Michael's daughter, Abbey, taking it easy with her dinner. She read the water and cast to this cagey trout.

Catching fish is an orchestrated effort—you must know what, where, and how.

Often, the edges of a steep bank are good places to cast.

water through their gills. If there's not a lot of oxygen in the water, it's uncomfortable for the fish, and they slow down accordingly. Perhaps the best analogy for us would be mountain climbing. There is a comfort zone for humans. As we start to push our comfort zone and climb higher into thinner air, we have to move slower and slower. A gulp of air at 16,000 feet is certainly not as satisfying as a gulp of air at sea level. We'd have to take seven or eight breaths to get the same effect as one at sea level.

Cool water holds oxygen better than warm water. The ideal temperature range for a given species is largely determined by how effectively the fish takes oxygen.

Dave often takes a trip to Clear Lake in Idaho for a little spring fishing. When the water is cool, the fish are active and healthy. They fight hard and are stratified throughout the water. One time in the summer, he stopped at Clear Lake to drop a line on the way back from Sun Valley. The fish were literally stacked up around the feeder creek trying to take in the cooler, more oxygenated water. When he hooked into one, even a good-size fish, there was little fight. The warm water and the lack of oxygen during this especially dry year had taken its toll.

Oxygen is also helpful for bug life. That is why you'll often find good fishing in riffles, which are very oxygenated waters. The fish won't hang here for long, but they view it as excellent hunting grounds. Stone flies are a classic bug that requires a lot of oxygen. When the stone fly hatch is on, successful anglers focus on oxygenated waters.

The Types of Water

We've talked about a number of things a fly angler has to keep in mind when he or she looks at a stretch of water. You have to understand the fish: what the fish eats, where it feels safe, and what makes it comfortable.

Now let's put another piece of the puzzle together. Let's look at the types of water you will encounter.

Streams and Rivers

A body of moving water can be divided into *pools, runs, riffles,* and *flats.* When you fly fish, it's important to know how each of these function and how to fish them.

Pools. A pool is a slow, deep hole that generally holds the biggest fish in the water. Fish can easily feed at the head or the tail of the pool, and they can lie dormant in the middle in the deepest water, where it's safe. Pools are often the most ideal lies because they meet so many of the fish's needs. It's no surprise that the largest fish—fish that have played King of the Hill successfully—have staked this water out.

Runs. A run is an even-flowing body of water. The top is generally smooth with occasional swirls because the bottom is frequently broken up by rocks and other structure. From the surface the water looks flat, but the bottom offers plenty of hiding places even though the water isn't deep. A run will meet many of the fish's needs. The structure breaks up the current, and there's a place to hide while resting or feeding. The water also has plenty of oxygen. Active fish find runs to be good feeding waters. The rocks and vegetation are excellent for insect life. The water gets a lot of sun, and things fish like to eat can be found here.

Riffles. Think of a riffle as a flowing cafeteria. The water is from 1 to 3 feet deep, and the top is broken and choppy. There is a lot of aquatic life. Active fish can often be found in the riffles. Surprisingly, a lot of anglers overlook this part of the stream. Fishing here can be quite exciting. Because the water is moving fast, fish have to react quickly. A fly caster in this water gets a lot of fast action. While the water isn't deep, the broken surface gives

This fine fish was caught in the riffles. It was in a feeding zone and took a hopper pattern even though it was late in the fall.

Beaver ponds can be home for large fish. Look for structure and places a fish can hide.

fish a sense of confidence, and they aren't skittish. Fish will come to the surface quickly and have a very splashy rise since they must act so quickly.

Flats. A flat is shallow, smooth water. There is little protection for the fish, so when fish come into the flats to feed, they will be very spooked. Fish come into a flat and feed heavily during a hatch. The angler who fishes here has to be very careful not to startle the prey. Even the wake from your waders—let alone the sight of you or your shadow—will send fish for the far reaches of the pool. Long, light leaders and flies with parachute patterns are the norm.

Ponds and Lakes

The secret to fly fishing ponds and lakes is to look for edges or seams. Fish can be anywhere, but the successful caster won't fish at random. The successful angler fishes with a plan and starts where he or she thinks the fish are most likely to be.

There is protection in the depths, and there is food in the shallows. Look for places where deep and shallow water come together. It's easier for large fish to come into the shallows from the deeper water.

Moss lines are excellent places since they provide homes for a variety of insects and smaller fish. Sandy bottoms aren't good places; look for where there are rocks, fallen trees, snags, and other structures that offer hiding places. Bugs and small fish thrive in such areas. Large fish like these places for the bugs and because they can ambush smaller fish.

In reservoirs, the old streambed is a good place to start. Michael loves to fish Gooseberry Reservoir in the Manti Mountains in Utah. The action can be fast or slow—depending on whether you know where the old stream channel is. The best fish hang out in the old streambed. If you get your fly near the bed, be ready for action. If you don't, pack a book and read.

Don't overlook streams that feed into the lake. Besides bringing in fresh food, streams attract to fish because they provide excellent oxygen.

It's important to go where the fish are. On ponds and lakes, a canoe can help get the caster to the fish.

5

KNOWING YOUR BUGS

The Study of Entomology

Fly casters need to know a little bit about the flies they're imitating.

It's necessary that you understand something about the nature of the bugs (or, more properly, the insects) so critical to a fish's life and to angling success. The discipline is technically called *entomology,* a fancy word for the investigation of insects. So hang on while we take a quick course in bugs. Besides casting, this may be the most confusing part of fly fishing. For most of us, bugs look a lot like . . . bugs. Until now, most of us haven't given much thought to the subject except for an occasional swat and a curse.

When a new caster takes a look at entomology, he or she might feel a growing panic. Can I learn all this stuff? It seems so overwhelming. The answer is yes, you can. This isn't a college course, nor do you need to pursue a degree in bug science. For most of us, a rudimentary understanding of entomology is all any caster needs. You need a basic understanding of the major bugs a fish might find appetizing (as well as the basic habits and stages of development).

Let's take a look at the fundamentals. We will give you a working knowledge so you'll know what to tie on your tippet. For most successful fly casters, an overview is plenty. If you'd like to learn the Latin

Knowing your insects means a lot more fishing action. You can give the fish what they want.

How do you know what fly to tie on? It's a bit confusing. Select the fly to best match what the fish are feeding on.

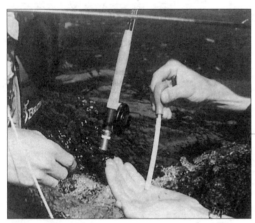

A good way to find out what the fish are taking is to take a sample and look at the contents.

terms and all the various subspecies and substages, you'll need to consult some dry college text. Our idea is to give you what is required to catch fish, lots of fish. You need a working awareness of the subjects you'll be imitating—but you don't need to live with them.

Before we look at specific insects, there are several things you ought to know concerning how fly casters go about the process of identifying them.

How to Pick Your Bug

You need to know what sorts of bugs you are up against so you can match them from your fly box. Sometimes it's hard to tell by just watching the air. You'll probably want to buy or make some sort of insect net so you can take samples from the water. It's pretty hard to collect specimens without it.

Once you've taken a sample, you'll want to consider three factors: *size, silhouette,* and *color.* This way you can accurately match the hatch with a fly you have in your box.

Size. This is probably the most important thing you'll need to consider when fishing an imitative pattern. Since you've collected a sample, you can accurately select a fly in your box that is the same size as the sample. When you match the hatch, size is your first consideration. Let's say that again since it's so critical: *Size is your first consideration.*

Silhouette. Determine the basic *shape* of the bug. Look at the wings first. Are they held upright or flat against the body? Are the wings still or active? The shape of the wings will help you make a basic identification. Also, there are variations among members of a species, and you want to account for such differences or at least be aware of them.

Color. This is least important of the three factors, but it shouldn't be ignored. Look at the underside of the bug, because this is what the fish sees. Don't worry about exact color; worry more about *light, medium,* and *dark.* If you have exact colors, match them; otherwise, go with a more general shade.

The reason you need to know these things is that you need to select the right fly. A few minutes spent netting samples will pay off quickly since you're more likely to present a fly the fish will be interested in. You'll be casting with a plan, not casting randomly. You will be fishing with a good idea about what the fish wants since you have matched the pattern accurately.

Another factor in helping you determine what they are eating is knowing the various ways fish feed. This is most apparent when you look at how they are breaking or affecting the surface film. For example, are the trout after nymphs, emergers, or adults? Do they gulp, sip, splash, or go airborne after their prey? You can get a good idea about what food they are after by looking carefully at dining habits.

Looking at how fish are lunching, coupled with samples you've collected, will give you an accurate idea about which bugs the trout are interested in at the moment. You can home in and be exact.

Perhaps when you've netted samples, you have a number of emergers and duns (we'll explain these terms in the section on mayflies). What should you tie on? It appears that you could successfully go with either pattern. Should you tie on the imitation of a dun or of an emerger? Looking at how the fish are feeding will give you a more exact clue. *If in doubt, fish the emerger.* This information will be a useful key in helping you match the hatch and plan a casting strategy. Learning how fish take certain species of insects (or stages of insects) will help you become a more successful fly caster. These first decisions when you get streamside often separate the average caster from the the one who catches lots of fish.

Now let's take a look at some specific insects.

An angler screens the water to find out what the conveyer belt is offering.

The Mayfly

The mayfly makes great trout food.

Mayflies Are King

A mayfly is the classic dry fly, the fly everyone calls "the little sailboat."

The *upright wings* of this fly, along with its *long skinny tail,* make the comparison apt. The mayfly really looks like a sailboat. This is the jewel among traditional flies (the first insect a fly tier probably tries to imitate).

When we look at this fly, we need to consider its different stages: nymphs, emergers, duns, and spinners. We will talk about the mayfly in some detail since this little bug is very important.

Nymphs

Different kinds of mayfly nymphs go through different nymph phases in the water. The most common are *crawlers, burrowers,* and *clingers.* Nymphs can be vulnerable to fish. Since we know that fish feed on the bottom more often than on the top, the nymph stage translates into fishing action for the wet-fly caster.

Crawlers are the most obvious, and this nymph is easily gulped down by the fish since they live on and around the rocks. They are exposed to the fish, especially when they are swept downstream by the current. Burrowers are buried in the mud and muck and are not as accessible. Clingers cling to anything they can.

To identify the nymphs, kick over rocks and debris downstream; collect samples with your insect net. Determine size, shape, and color of what you find. Remember, when fishing wets, fish aren't usually as selective as they are on the film.

The Flies to Use: Our favorites are the Pheasant Tail, the A. P. Nymph, and the Gold-Ribbed Hare's Ear.

Emergers

This is the next stage of the nymph's life.

This is when the nymph travels toward the surface to "hatch" again and when it's very vulnerable to predators. The tasty traveling nymph is preyed upon most heartily. When you happen upon an emergence, there can be exciting fishing. Trout feed to excess at such a time. The emerging stage is often overlooked by casters.

Catch emergers with your insect net. Scoop the water below the surface or deeper for samples.

As the nymph hits the film (the surface of the water), it starts to shed its husk. When the nymph breaks loose from its husk, the mature insect (called a *dun*) is born. At this stage, it's quite helpless. Fish prey on it with a vengeance. At such a time, the fish can be very selective since they key in on this insect and nothing else.

Look at how the fish are feeding. Fish will make a bulge on the surface, not leaving a bubble on the film, when they are feeding on emergers. Often the dorsal fin will be all that breaks the film.

Frequently, the fish will take the emerger and the surface insect concurrently. Nevertheless, an emerger will often work all the way through the hatch. In other words, an emerger will still work even though other stages of hatch are present.

The Flies to Use: Pheasant Tails are Michael's fly of choice for this stage (keep various sizes on hand). Dave ties up what he calls the Card Emerger, a fly with foam wings and a trailing husk. It's worth its weight in gold on a trout stream.

Duns

The dun is *the* classic dry-fly pattern. The word *dun* alone in some fishing circles is enough to get fly casters to forsake six-figure incomes and head for the nearest trout stream.

After the mayfly emerger comes to the surface and molts, the dun is born. The dun is easy to spot

The Callibaetis is a great still-water mayfly.

The Adams is very versatile.

because it has the definitive mayfly shape: long upright wings (the sailboat look) and a long skinny tail. The dun is called a *dun* because its wings are a dun color. The wings are translucent (when it becomes sexually mature, the wings will be clear and the fly will become darker). After the dun's wings have dried enough so it can fly, it will take off for nearby trees and bushes preparatory to mating. Sometimes birds will give you a clue about where a *hot* hatch is taking place. Our feathered friends feed heavily during such times. Notice how the birds act next time you are in a mayfly hatch.

On cool, cloudy days, the mayfly dun will sometimes float along the surface, perhaps batting its wings, waiting for them to dry. (It can't fly when they're wet.) When this happens, the fish feed heavily and become very specific feeders because they can key in on this stage. On sunny days or when it's warm, the dun's wings dry faster, so it flies sooner. At times like this, fish usually aren't feeding as specifically since they don't have as long to key in on one stage or shape.

Even after you have identified the hatch as mayfly dun, use your insect net to take some samples. As usual, you'll want to match the size, silhouette, and color (in that order).

Find a fly in your box that is the right size—or as close to the right size as you've got. If you are going to err on size, go smaller (going smaller is always better than going larger when it comes to selective fish). If you notice that fish are coming up and looking at your fly but not taking it, your fly is probably too large. Go down a size. Even if the color is wrong, it's better to go smaller.

Look at the bottom of the bug—which is what the fish sees—for color. Exact color isn't that critical. Worry more about getting in the ballpark: light, medium, or dark.

Fish take duns differently from emergers. You can easily tell. A fish going for a dun will stick its nose out of the water, leaving a bubble on the surface.

Fish may take duns at a dead drift. Let the current give the fly all the action. Your fly should ride just like the naturals that are riding the drift. *There should be no drag!*

The Flies to Use. The Adams #12 to #20 is almost everyone's favorite fly for the dun hatch. Next would be the Blue Wing Olive #16 to #20 (which Michael is very fond of) and the Pale Morning Dun #12 to #18 (Dave's favorite). These three patterns in a variety of sizes will cover the bases nearly all the time; they are the standards we always have in our fly boxes. Be aware that there are a thousand different patterns out there. Some variations might fit some waters better than others, so check with your local fly shop. Nevertheless, with what we have mentioned, you can successfully fish a dun hatch anywhere.

The Blue Wing Olive with a sponge wing.

Spent Spinners

After the mayfly has mated, it falls to the water. It is now called a *spent spinner.* A spinner has the same basic body shape as the dun, but it will be a little bit thinner and shinier. The wings will be a clear light dun (or clear and speckled), laid back flat on the water (not up like a sailboat).

The fish will feed very slowly and deliberately at this stage. Fish will cruise the back eddies and non-chalantly take from the film. Fish will be hard to see because they ride low in the water. A good pair of *polarized glasses are an absolute must.* (Michael has his regular prescription glasses polarized.) It's easy to lose your fly in the glare on the water. Sometimes you have to guess where the fly is and lift your rod tip if a fish rises. Otherwise, it will take and spit your fly before you've had a chance to set the hook.

The Flies to Use: Fish any spent-wing pattern (such as the Rusty Dun Spinner) #12 to #20, in a variety of colors depending on the location. A rust-bodied fly with light blue wings will cover the majority of spinner falls. A black-bodied fly with a white wing is another standby.

The Caddis Fly

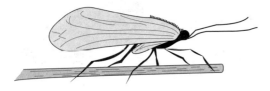

The Chamois Caddis.

Caddis Flies

You'll grow to love caddis flies. The caddis fly is the most plentiful aquatic bug, and the caddis family is the largest of all the aquatic-bug families. Luckily, the variations are pretty similar, so you don't have to carry a huge selection of patterns to match the hatch. Fishing the caddis is a little more forgiving than the mayfly.

Caddis flies look like *little pup tents*—little pup tents with mothlike wings laid back along their bodies when they rest. These little critters are often mistaken for moths (the sort that buzz around your lantern when you're camping). The antennae are long and pronounced.

Nymphs

Most of us are familiar with the type of caddis nymph—sometimes referred to as a rock roller—that builds little houses on the bottom of rocks in streams. But there are a number of nymph varieties, or larvae, and they look a lot alike. Some are free-living; some build rock houses (rock rollers); some live in watery, spiderlike webs; and some live in the mud.

Disturb the bottom of the stream (or look under rocks) and try to net several samples. Compare them with the criteria we have discussed and match to the proper size, shape, and color in selecting the fly to fish with.

The Flies to Use: Flies you might consider are the Chamois Caddis #12 to #18, the Muskrat Nymph #12 to #18, the Fur Nymph #12 to #18, Serendipity #16 to #20 (Dave's favorite), and the Gold-Ribbed Hare's Ear #12 to #18 (Mike's favorite), in various colors. Fish the larval stage at a dead drift near the bottom so the fly tumbles with the current. You're trying to simulate a larva that has been dislodged.

Emergers

An emerging caddis is here and gone.

The caddis larva will make a cocoon much like a butterfly. It will develop until it's ready and then break out. There is no delay. When it's ready, it rushes to the surface. Unlike the mayfly, which needs to pause and dry its wings, the caddis will often break the surface film and burst into flight without any sign of delay.

When fish are taking caddis emergers, the rises are very splashy as the fish chases the insect. Sometimes, fish leap completely out of the water. The rise is very exciting, so try not to lift too hard when you set the hook. Try to remain calm.

The Flies to Use: A caster will want to have the LaFontain Sparkle Caddis #10 to #16 on hand to match this stage of the hatch. There are a number of flies you could use, but this one is our first choice. Fish the emerger patterns with some action or at a dead drift. Try both ways and see which works best. Fish will often hit an emerging caddis with gusto as it is swimming toward the surface. Many times a fish in dead backwater will rush to a fly as it is lifted from a rest on the bottom of the pool and brought up toward the surface.

Adults

After mating is completed, the adult caddis will return to the water to lay eggs. At this time they scoot across the surface in a frenetic manner. Some species will dive under the water to lay their eggs; others deposit their eggs on the surface.

You may hear a caster talk about "skating" a fly across the film. This means he or she is working the fly to look like an active egg-laying caddis. This is one time you will want to work your fly and not just

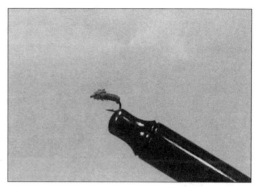

The Serendipity.

The Gold-Ribbed Hare's Ear is one of the most important flies you can have in your fly box.

The Goddard Caddis.

The Stone Fly

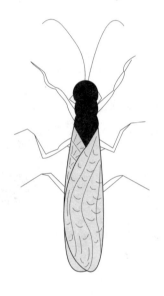

Rubber-legged adult stone fly.

have it dead drift. It's also a time when a little drag on your fly might be a positive thing. It must be controlled, however. Calculated twitches and little dances might trigger a response. Too much, and you'll alarm your prey.

Trout will be very active on an adult caddis hatch. They will make bold leaps and often break the water with bravado. It is exciting to watch.

Flies to Use: Probably the best pattern, and certainly a favorite, is the Elk Hair Caddis #12 to #16. Fish it at a dead drift, or skate it across the water in an active manner. Another good pattern is the Goddard Caddis #12 to #16 fished the same way. Soft Hackle Wets are good imitations of diving caddis. You can fish these on a swing and then strip.

Stone Flies

As you would imagine, stone flies hang around rocky areas. They like fast-moving water.

Stone flies, sometimes called salmon flies, are the favorites of many casters. During the stone fly hatch, more marriages are strained, more bosses threaten firings, and more lawns go unmowed than at any other time of the year. The timing of this blessed event will vary depending on where you live. Wherever that may be, stone flies are a lot of fun. There are several stages we need to consider.

Nymphs: Black and Brown

Nymphs can be brown or black. They live in the water up to a year before hatching. They are very active crawling about the rocks. Fish will pick them off the rocks if the occasion presents itself. However, most often the nymph is swept away by the current and is defenseless.

The Flies to Use: Patterns that will be useful are the Box Stone, the Bitch Creek (wonder where these guys have fished?), and the Kaufman Stone in sizes

#4 to #12. Fish nymphs at a dead drift so the fly occasionally bumps the bottom (do this by adjusting the shot to the current). It is very important that you get the pattern scuttling across the bottom with the current.

Emergers

When the stone fly emerges, it crawls its way over the bottom to the shore, a log, or a handy rock. It's a very exposed bug at this time. Fish this fly the same way you'd fish the nymph stage. The actual emergence occurs on the bank.

Adults: Orange and Yellow

Orange and yellow are the key colors for the adult stone fly. The stone fly is a large, winged insect. It has two tails and conspicuous antennae. Their gills are between their legs. Most noticeably, they feature a double wing case. They're also predators in their own right, feasting on nymphs and other aquatic stuff. Stone flies fly about and sooner or later return to the water to lay eggs.

The Flies to Use: A Simulator or an Elk Hair Caddis is Dave's first choice for matching an adult stone fly. Fish stone flies at a dead drift. If that doesn't produce results, fish at a dead drift and periodically twitch the fly to feign a struggling insect on the surface film.

Midges: The Small Bug

In the last few years, almost any small bug has been called a midge. A fly caster talking about a midge hatch may be referring to a specific insect or to any sort of similar-looking diminutive bug.

The key word is *small*.

Remember all those swarms of bugs that seemed to hatch by the millions and millions and that

An excellent stone fly imitation—a Dave Card special.

Stone fly nymph with seal fur.

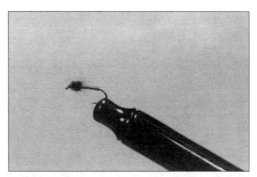

The Brassie is an excellent wet fly. Every caster should have several.

looked like flying grains of sand? They didn't sting but just swarmed about and made a general nuisance of themselves. When you slapped, you killed about seventy-two at once. You get the picture. Because there are so many, a fish can get very plump gorging itself on the swarms. The amount of energy expended to gulp a single fly or two wouldn't be worth it. But when there are millions, it's another story. When fish are feeding on midges, they get very selective and very fat.

In a collective way, let's look at midge stages.

Nymphs

Midge nymphs are small, wormlike larvae that frequent the weeds. What they lack in size, they make up for in numbers. When the nymph is active, the fish are greedy.

The Flies to Use: You can imitate this bug with a Brassie #16 to #20, or with a Serendipity #16–#20 (all colors). Fish at a dead drift. Repeat, it must be a drag-free, dead drift.

An insect screen will be your best friend. You can find out what is floating in the current.

Emergers

After the larva has matured, it will "emerge" or break away to the surface. During the emerging process and on the surface, it will be very vulnerable to preying fish. Such fish will bulge on the surface and rise many times a minute to feed on these tiny morsels.

The Flies to Use: You can catch fish at this time with a Kimble Emerger #20 to #24 or a Griffiths Gnat (trim bottom of fly) #18 to #22. Fish at a dead drift.

Adults

This is the stage most of us think of when we say midge. These diminutive bugs have two wings and the basic shape of a mosquito.

Sometimes there seems to be literally millions of bugs on the water. The fish are frenzied, and your blood will be running hot, too. The midges will be very active on the surface, and fish will be feasting.

The Flies to Use: To improve your odds of catching a fine lunker, fish some of Dave's favorites, the Double Ugly #12 to #16 or the Griffiths Gnat #18 to #22. Fish will feed slowly but steadily. Dead drift on the film.

Terrestrials in the Water

Few things are more tasty to a fish than a yummy terrestrial—such as a grasshopper, beetle, or cricket. And since the earth-going insects are usually large, there's a lot of energy consumed for the effort spent. The wind or a careless step often causes such bugs to fall in the water.

Some casters spend their warm-weather fishing lives casting only terrestrials and never get to other patterns since they are so busy hauling in lunker after lunker. Fish seem to love them, and they are fun to fish with.

Every fly box ought to have a collection of terrestrials. Each area will require you to tune your selection in size and color to the local populations.

The Flies to Use:

• Ants: black and brown, #14 to #18
• Grasshoppers, #6 to #12
• Beetles: black and brown, #12 to #16
• Cicada: black and brown, #6 to #10
• Crickets: black, #8 to #12

Fish these patterns on a dead drift with an occasional twitch to indicate a struggle. The actual creatures are helpless in the current, but they'll fight it as long as they have energy. A struggling bug is a dinner bell to a fish. The fish can take such an insect slowly and deliberately or in a swooping blast. If nothing is obviously hatching and you see fish periodically taking something on the surface, try a terrestrial pattern.

The extended Green Drake is a tempting fly.

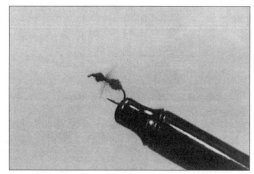

The ant is a tasty trout bite and is a must for your tackle box.

The beetle is an important fly to have in your trout box.

A close-up of scuds screened from a river.

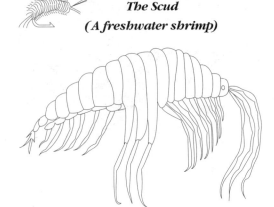

The Scud
(A freshwater shrimp)

Scuds: Freshwater Shrimp

These little freshwater shrimp look a little bit like a pill bug. Trout will go out of their way to munch on them. Almost any place there are weeds, there will be scuds. Sometimes they get dislodged from their weedy home and tumble down the river. A trout that finds a free-floating scud usually takes it.

Fish will sometimes plunge into the moss to knock scuds loose. Impatient fish will even nudge at rocks to break loose a scud stuck in the cracks. On occasions you'll see millions of scuds drifting along with the current and creating an underwater feeding frenzy.

An essential part of your wet-fly fishing arsenal will be the scud. If you never tied on another fly and fished with scuds for the rest of your life, you'd often have a smile on your face. You'd be catching fish. A few patterns in several sizes, #12 to #18, are a must for your fly box.

The Flies to Use: Trout love scuds; it's one of Michael's favorite flies. The most important thing is to match the size. Getting the right color is nice but not as important.

Worms

Worms actually live in the water—in the tailwater, the water at the end of the pool, in particular. They look like small garden worms, but they are mostly in shades of amber, red, and brown.

Folks who fly fish sometimes look down on worm fishers. Well, actually, on bait fishers in general. There's something about that stiff upper lip and doing it on a fly or nothing. But there are times you'll want to use a worm. Not live ones, however. We're talking about fishing flies that mimic worm patterns.

The Flies to Use: Every now and then, it's really fun to tie on a worm pattern and give it a drift. The fly we have found successful is the San Juan Worm pattern. There are a number of variations on this pattern. We don't suggest you fill your fly box with worms, but a few are handy to have.

Crayfish

All species of freshwater fish will eat crayfish. Dave once found five small crayfish in the stomach of a fish he was cleaning. Armed with the knowledge that the lunkers were on a crayfish feed, Dave put on an attractor crayfish-pattern fly, plunged into the water, and started to catch more than his fair share of fish. Michael couldn't understand why Dave was suddenly so successful. It wasn't until late afternoon that Dave let the "cray out of the bag" and let Michael in on the secret.

The Flies to Use: You can use an actual crayfish pattern to imitate a large cray. If you're after larger trout or smallmouth bass, this will be a successful pattern. For most of us who occasionally want to imitate this creature, a Brown or Olive Wooly Bugger will do the trick.

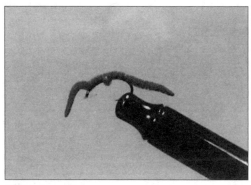

The San Juan Worm.

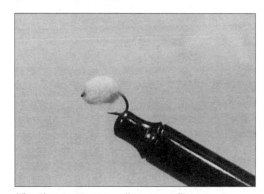

The Glow Bug is an excellent spawn fly.

6

PUTTIN' ON THE GLITZ

Attracting Patterns

Attracting patterns have a wonderful niche in the world of fly fishing. They are flies that work effectively on fish, but they don't seem to "imitate" any sort of natural insect in particular. An attracting pattern is a *generic* presentation of *something* that appears to look like food to a fish, but it's just a made-up pattern. Maybe it's a composite of several insects.

When you first start casting, you're trying to remember to keep tight lines, to keep your loops hook-shaped and small, to hit the water softly with your line—and then you're also trying to match the hatch in selecting the fly to use. That's a lot to remember. As you are juggling all these concepts at once, *attracting-pattern flies can be your best friends because they catch fish and you don't have to worry about trying to imitate a specific insect.*

Attracting patterns give you something to start with while you're absorbing the more complicated elements of learning to match your fly to a specific hatch. With an attracting pattern, you don't have to worry about exactness.

Let's look at attracting patterns and see what they are, how they work, and which basic patterns you'll find useful. We'll examine them for both trout and warm-water species.

Here's an excellent rainbow taken on a Wooly Worm, a wet-fly attracting pattern all anglers should carry.

Notice the spots on this attractive trout.

Fishing in the middle of the stream—with a fish on.

Why Attracting Patterns?

In the last chapter, we spent a lot of time talking about exact hatches and how to match your fly to what the fish are eating at the moment. Matching the hatch is probably the best way to land lots of fish, but it can take time. And we must confess there can be frustrating moments. When you are trying to keep your line out of the bushes, it's nice not to have to worry about fly selection.

On days when you want to focus on improving your cast and don't want to be changing a fly every few minutes—or when you just want to fish and not be bothered—a good attracting pattern that you can tie on and leave on might be just the way to go. It will free you up so you can concentrate on other things—like not snagging the willows or simply enjoying the day. Besides, sometimes it's fun to bust into a stream and work your way up with a Wulff or an Adams.

Perhaps an equally valid reason to learn about attracting patterns is the fact that there will come times when, even with all you understand about entomology, you still can't figure out what the fish want or what the fish are feeding on. You can't match the hatch with any pattern in your box. Perhaps you have a fly close to what they are taking, but they won't even look at it. Or maybe you're on vacation and you're fishing in a region new to you. You can't know all the local favorites.

Michael was in Alaska a few years ago, fishing for trophy rainbow trout. He arrived after the local fly shop had closed, but there was still enough light in the land of the midnight sun for a few precious hours of fishing. Not one to sit about his room in a fishing paradise, Mike broke out his rod and hit the water.

Several specific flies were known to be very deadly on that stream; in fact, it was said that if you weren't using the local favorites, you weren't going to catch anything but driftwood. Michael knew the

The Basic Fly

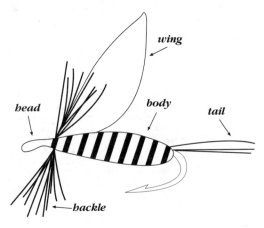

specific patterns but didn't have time to tie a batch up before he left Utah. Anxiously, he tried everything in his box that was similar, without success.

After an hour of watching big trout do everything but take his fly, he tied on an attracting pattern, a #12 Royal Coachman, and took one nice fish. He lost several others before it got dark. The Coachman wasn't as good as the "proven" patterns, but at least he was fishing and enjoying some success. A box of attractors saved his evening.

How Attracting Patterns Work

No one is really sure how attracting patterns work, but they do. The concept is to attract a fish to the fly and have it take a bite.

An attracting pattern doesn't look like a specific fish food, a specific fly, but it does look like food in general. The fish aren't exactly sure what it is either, but if the pattern looks good enough to eat, they might take a bite. An expert's best guess is that attracting patterns look like a lot of yummy bugs rolled into one.

Fish can't test things with their fingers as people do; they do their testing with their mouths. An attracting pattern works by triggering something in the fish, making it want to take a sample bite. Some materials have proven very dependable in these patterns, such as peacock herl. This vivid feather gives off a translucent, buggy look that fish can't seem to resist, in both wet and dry patterns. This fly is dressed up to attract.

The Royal Wulff.

Where to Start

As you start to build up your fly box, attracting patterns are some of the first flies you ought to collect. We've selected five wet and five dry patterns to give you a good working base. You'll note that some flies are specific imitator patterns (like the Muddler and

The Royal Coachman is one of the best and most beloved attracting patterns.

The Humpy is a great attractor fly. It is a good fly to start with if you aren't sure what to use.

the Adams). Also, some patterns can be fished both wet or dry (like the Renegade, Wulff, and Coachman). These ten flies will allow you to fish successfully almost anywhere. Michael is a big Coachman fan. It's his favorite attractor. (He caught his first fish on this fly, and it holds sentimental value.) Dave is a big Wulff fan since he feels it rides better in the water. Michael rarely uses a Wulff and Dave rarely uses a Coachman. But they both work very well.

Some of the patterns we recommend come with different color variations. You might want to check with a shop or a seasoned caster in your area to see if one color seems to work better than another so you can acquire it first. Eventually, you may want the pattern in several color phases. The following flies are not necessarily listed in order of their importance:

Attracting Patterns You Should Carry

Dry Flies

- Humpy #10 to #16 (color phases)
- Royal Wulff #10 to #16 (fished wet or dry)
- Royal Coachman #14 to #20 (fished wet or dry)
- Renegade #10 to #18 (fished wet or dry)
- Adams #12 to #20

Wet Flies

- Prince Nymph #12 to #16
- Hare's Ear #12 to #16
- Gray Hackle Peacock #12 to #16
- Wooly Worm/Bugger #6 to #8
- Muddler Minnow #6 to #10

Attracting Patterns to Add Later

After you get started on the basics, there are other attracting-pattern flies you may want to collect. For dry flies, you could use the Mosquito, the Irresistible, the White Wulff, the Madam X, and the Double Humpy. For wet flies, add the Tellico, the Zug Bug, the Martinez, and the Pheasant Tail. And, as Michael says, you can't have enough Hare's Ears.

How to Fish Attracting Patterns

You'll usually fish an attracting fly the same way you would a specific fly.

Dry. With dry flies, you will generally dead drift your fly over the area where you think the fish are lying. If you are fishing through dead or still water, and you haven't been able to pull a rise from a fish, you can try an occasional twitch to attract the fish's attention. This simulates a struggling insect on the surface fighting the current. But don't overdo it. A good twitch now and then will work wonders. One too many twitches, and you can forget about catching a thing.

Wet. Wet flies are fished both dead drift and actively retrieved. Experiment with the dead drift and the retrieve. As a rule of thumb, big fish often are attracted to more active prey. Wooly Buggers, Wooly Worms, and Muddlers are excellent patterns to animate with a twitch or a strip. (In fast water you'll probably want to dead drift these patterns.)

The famous Wooly Worm.

Ideas on Trout and Warm-Water Fish

Trout

Trout generally take small bites, so you'll use small flies. A trout takes a fly gracefully and fights like a freight train. A trout nibbles. Trout like to look at their food, so the dead drift or having a fly sitting on the film will work very well. The patterns we've introduced so far in this chapter are designed primarily for trout. They will work on all game fish, however, including bass.

This Gray Hackle wet is a great fly to start with.

A Mohair Leech is a good pattern for trophy fish.

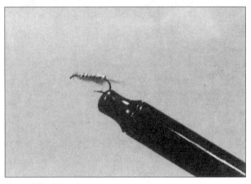

A modified Scud pattern.

This nice brown took a #20 pink Scud.

Bass

A bass takes the fly like a freight train, then fights like two freight trains. It gulps. An eight-pound largemouth can take in almost a quart of water during a single gulp. When you fish for bass, you must fish the fly actively. Bass like their food moving. The secret with largemouth is more in *how* you fish the fly and not so much in the fly itself.

Bass casting is the fastest-growing segment of fly fishing. Many anglers are just discovering how much fun a bass can be on a fly rod. While we worship the trout, we're also bass fans who've caught boatloads of largemouth on every fly suggested thus far. They work quite well.

There are also excellent bass flies meant specifically for the wily largemouth. You'll want to collect them if you do much bass fishing. You'll find these attracting-pattern flies useful:

- Leech (Marabou; black, white, red, yellow; weighted/unweighted) #6 to #14
- Muddler Minnow #1/0 to #10
- Hopper #4 to #12
- Popper (deer hair) #6 to #12
- Water Pup #6 to #8

Depending on where you live, you might want to add crayfish, sculpin, and minnow patterns. (While often thought of as attracting patterns, crayfish can be fairly specific, too.)

Panfish

The fly suggestions we've made for bass will also be successful on panfish. Don't worry about crossing over. But if you are going to do a lot of panfishing, you'll want to add a few flies to those we've mentioned. Patterns that have yellow in them seem especially good. You might consider:

- Sponge Spider #8 to #12
- Popper (deer hair) #10 to #14

- Mickey Finn Bucktail (weighted/unweighted) #8 to #12
- Wooly Bugger (black, weighted) #8 to #12
- Leech (Marabou; black, white, red, yellow; weighted/unweighted) #8 to #14
- Leadwing Coachman (weighted/unweighted) #10 to #16
- Hopper #8 to #14

In addition to these flies, consider other streamers, both Bucktail and Marabou, in a variety of colors and sizes. You may also want to add the Zug Bug, the Water Beetle, the Crayfish, and the Hellgrammite Nymph.

Michael likes to fish for panfish with weighted flies. Dave prefers to fish them unweighted and weight the leader. He feels a weighted fly affects the action and that it's better to weight the line. Michael feels that for panfish, it doesn't matter.

The flies we recommend for panfish pop the top of the water quite well, which you'll often want to do when casting for panfish. You'll want to fish them more actively than you would trout.

Releasing a fine fish.

7

PUTTING YOUR BEST FLY FORWARD

The Fishing Plan and Mending

Presentation is the most important part of casting.

To be successful, your fly has to be perfectly displayed (or the fish has to be in a very hungry mood) if you are going to get any fishing action. A fly must always look natural; it must drift realistically; it must look similar to the fish's regular food (or, at the very least, look foodlike).

In this chapter we'll discuss how to look at the water so you can fish with a *plan*. We will also talk about how to adjust your line to get the best drift. This indispensable process is called *mending*.

Your Master Fishing Plan

Your master plan is your fishing strategy. Instead of blundering into the water and casting haphazardly, you will think before you act. You need to know the best way to get your fly to the wary fish. You have to fish the water effectively.

In this chapter, we will give you the blueprint for effectively casting with a purpose, so you can design a fishing plan for the water you're on.

The result of reading the water properly is catching fish.

Where do you start?

Thinking Ahead

Think think think before you throw your first cast or step into the water. Here's a scenario of how you might go about setting yourself up for a perfect cast. Consider this situation:

You're on the Big Bear River. The banks are lined with willows. You've stumbled into a hungry moose munching tender shoots on the path. When you look down, you notice grizzly tracks near the river. There's an excitement in the air as you quicken your pace and feel a hint of anxiety. At last you break through the forest, and you're on the stream. Standing in a shallow riffle about 10 inches deep, you note the river is about 50 feet wide, clear and cold.

Upstream you see a rock in the middle of the current 100 feet away; a lively cutthroat has broken the surface. There are a couple of snags, one near the bank, the other almost directly in front of the rock. It looks like the water behind the rock is at least 3 or 4 feet deep. Since the rock breaks the flow nicely, it appears to be a likely place for fish to hold with nice seams on both sides. You're so excited to fish you can hardly stand it. But you stop and think first, asking yourself several questions:

- *Where am I going to start casting?*
- *How close can I get before I spook the fish?*
- *What spot looks like the best water for hiding fish?*
- *Will I cast to the best spot first or cast to the fringes and work inward?*
- *Will casting to one pool foul or spook another pool or eddy?*

Other questions may come to mind as you work out your plan of attack. What about the fallen log that's on the close left by the sandbar? What about the big rocks in the ankle-deep water in front of you? What about the several conflicting currents between you and the rock 100 feet away that will pull at your line? And what of the several currents close to that rock that create the seams?

A successful fishing plan will depend on your thoughtful answers to the questions posed by the river. In the following pages, we'll look at some of the main considerations that go into creating your plan.

Current Considerations

Position yourself so you can avoid as many current problems as possible. You can't avoid all of them. It's nice if you can cast on water that is all flowing at the same pace; but this situation is, at best, occasional. Water is almost always flowing at different rates because of various factors, including structure on the bottom, merging currents, bends, and logs. To keep your fly drifting naturally through the current, you will have to do some line adjusting. This is called mending, and we'll pick this subject up later in the chapter.

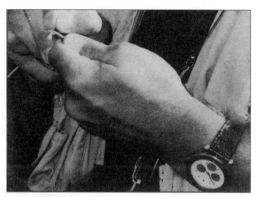

Before you tie on a fly, have a plan for fishing the water.

Most of the time when you are fishing, you are dealing with several different current speeds at once. You can't keep searching for that perfect place to cast where all the water is flowing in unison. It's the different rates of flow that make a water healthy for the fish it hosts. It creates seams.

Before you pounce in and cast, take a minute to analyze the currents. Examine the eddies and the flow of the water. What about the faster middle currents? Or the slower current on the edges? Know where each is and what each will do to your line and fly. It won't take long before you'll get a feel for your line and how it will react on water. Study the bubbles, foam, and driftwood. Notice which current takes the bubbles faster and notice where it takes the bubbles slower. See how the sandbar, the log, and rocks speed up and slow down the water.

After you've fished a section of water, do some homework. Throw your line out and see how it's moved by the different currents. See how some current causes the line to belly and the fly to drag.

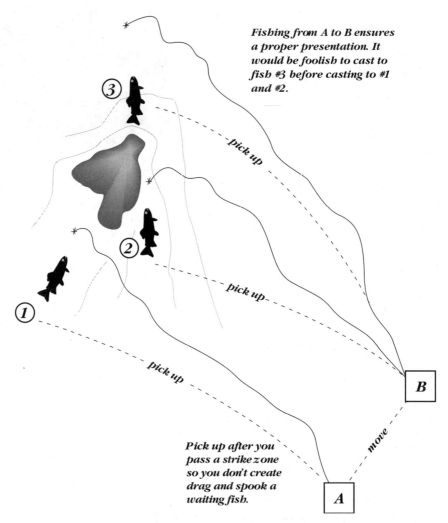

Fishing from A to B ensures a proper presentation. It would be foolish to cast to fish #3 before casting to #1 and #2.

pick up

pick up

pick up

move

Pick up after you pass a strike zone so you don't create drag and spook a waiting fish.

Fish with a strategy. Know what you are going to do before you make a move. First, decide where you will fish—then decide how. Try to avoid spooking fish waiting nearby.

Notice how the faster current bellies your line faster. How long does it take until your fly starts to drift unnaturally?

This may not be as much fun as fishing, but you can learn a lot by experimenting with your line on the current. Watch your line closely and see how it responds to the current.

It's important that you understand the water and especially the currents. Water doesn't all move at the same speed. It's influenced by the surroundings.

Rocks. The current goes around or over rocks depending on their size and location. The water slows behind the rock, making it good holding water. To some degree, the water is also slowed down to the front and the edges, making this good fishing water. The water also pillows in front of the rock, creating a good spot for a trout to rest from the speed of the current and to inspect any food that is delivered down the drift.

Dave carefully releasing this pint-size pike that was feeding in the weeds by the edge of the river.

Trees. Snags and logs slow the water, but it's not a complete blockage. This allows a break in the current where fish can rest. It also allows bugs to filter through. Snags are rich in bug life, but it can be very difficult to deliver a fly there since a fish will often put its nose very close to the logs. Do not pass these areas up, however, because they will often hold the wisest and, thus, the largest fish in a water system.

Eddies. This is where the current swirls in circles, holding the food longer. Fish will often face downstream and wait for the food to be circled up. Eddies are found at the back side of a rock or other obstruction. They are usually the most recognized fish-holding waters on a stream and thus are highly fished. But don't pass them up, because they can hold large numbers of very active fish.

Upstream or Downstream

Do you present your fly upstream, or downstream, or cast from the side? There is no right answer. Go where you will get the best drift; go where the fish are. Frequently you'll cast upstream or do a quartering cast (see the chapters on wet and dry flies). There are a number of casts to choose from.

Some beginning casters are told to cast only upstream and let the fly drift back to them. There's sound logic in this method. Having the line drift back to you is probably the easiest way to control

This excellent fish was caught behind a rock.

Cast to the upstream tip of the strike zone

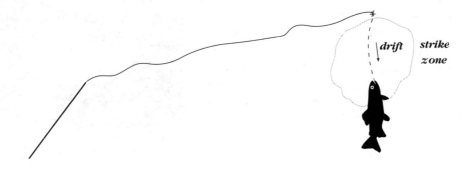

drift   *strike zone*

It is critical that your fly drift naturally through the strike zone. Cast your line to the top of the strike zone and mend to ensure a proper drift.

it—especially if the current is flowing somewhat uniformly. If the current is faster close to you, however, you'll have trouble with drag almost immediately, and you'll have to mend to keep the drift right. Our suggestion is to cast mostly upstream for the time being. You'll probably feel a little more comfortable and work the line better.

With a downstream cast, you can get your fly to the fish before your line. The problem is that it's harder to control your line. But every now and then take a good look at the stream and the current between you and the fish. If it looks like you can get a better drift by casting downstream, get out of the stream. Take a walk around the area so you won't spook the fish and get upstream. Then try some downstream casting. If you're careful, you'll be pleased with the results. Casting downstream can be very effective, and sometimes it's the best way to go. Don't ignore this important method of presentation.

Staying in Control

Cast so you're in control at all times. As simple as it sounds, stand where you're not likely to hang up on a back cast. You don't want to be so anxious that your first back cast takes fifteen minutes to untangle. We all do our share of untangling, but it takes away from time on the water. Every time you fish, remind yourself to look and see what's over your shoulder.

A Plan for Casting

If you see any fish activity, cast to the fish you see first. If you don't see any activity, cast to what you *think* is the best place first (that is, where the biggest fish will likely be). An exception in casting to the best water first would be if casting to such a spot might spook some other likely areas around it that you want to work later.

If the *best* area—in front of a rock, for example—produces a fish, you'll want to work the rest of the water in front of the rock *carefully*. The water in front of the rock often provides a buffer zone for feeding fish. If you can reach and accurately cast to the water in front of the rock before fishing the edges and in back, do it. If not, fish what you can and move up and work the top water.

By now, you know how far you can cast accurately. Don't try to overcast, because you're likely to foul some good water. Work within your casting zone. If you need to take a few steps to the right or left to work some of the edges, do it. Then move up a yard or so and work the water that you weren't able to reach.

The Spoilers

Cast to the best spots first as you work your way toward them. Be sure not to spoil any water as you progress. As the saying goes, "Cast to it before you spoil it!" The secret is to cover the water consistently and thoroughly. Give every fish on the prowl a chance to taste your fly.

It's a genuine education to sit by the streamside and watch other casters. It's sad that so many novice

Know why you are tying on the fly—the right fly is part of your fishing plan.

Sometimes you have to sneak up on a likely fish, being careful not to spoil other good spots along the way.

This fine trout was taken next to a sunken log.

Watch how your line moves in the water.

fly casters plunge into the current and start casting without thinking first, often spoiling likely fishing spots because they didn't have a plan.

One summer day on Utah's Green River, Dave noticed a group of eager beginning casters, apparently from the local fly fishing club or school, get out of a VW bus and literally hit the water. One over-anxious woman started fishing with a vengeance. After an hour she climbed out of the water and commented to Dave that the hole didn't seem very good and that the Green wasn't all that great.

Dave didn't tell her that he'd caught several good fish that morning in the same water. Dave had scouted the stream before fishing and had gone in about 35 yards below where the woman was now standing. His plan was to work upstream slowly and fish the side pockets and seams near the bank. He'd caught most of his fish within yards of where the woman was now.

But the unsuccessful caster had moved about carelessly, casting randomly. She'd plunged into the river without thought and started throwing flies. Instead of fishing the next pocket above her, she cast randomly about the water, missing the finest seams and holes. As she moved upstream, she stood in the best water and fished in the least productive manner.

We have all made such mistakes. We all had to start sometime. And every now and then, no matter how good we get, we're going to miscalculate and foul up some potentially good water. The secret is not doing it too often. Fish the good water, and stand in the not so good water. When you move up, stand in the good water you have already worked.

Mending Your Line

You've done everything you can to set yourself up right. You're fishing with a plan. Now let's learn how to control your line.

Line Behavior

We've learned that nearly all the time, you want your fly to float naturally with the drift of the current. We have learned that to get to productive lies where the fish might be holding or feeding, your line might cross several different currents. These currents act upon your line and have a direct effect upon your fly's drift. They can either help it or hurt it.

Different currents are obstacles. But there is nothing you can't handle. In fact, you can turn the situation to your advantage. Earlier in this chapter, we identified many of the current situations you are

Drag

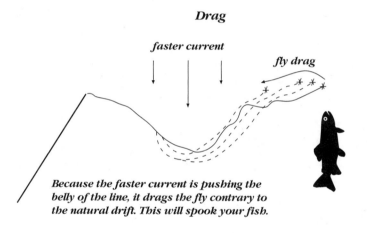

Because the faster current is pushing the belly of the line, it drags the fly contrary to the natural drift. This will spook your fish.

Mend to Correct Drag

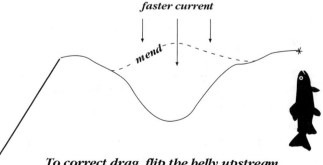

To correct drag, flip the belly upstream.

likely to come up against. Now let's talk about how to take the drag out of your presentation.

We will show you how to make your line behave so your fly will drift naturally—and, in turn, attract fish.

You need to manipulate your line so this happens. More often than not, fish will be in the slower waters on the fringes of the current. You need to get your fly to float without drag for the longest possible time.

Your fly will only do what your line tells it to do! Remember, you are the one in control.

Yes, you are in control—not the current. When we discussed casting, we said that your line will do what your rod tip tells it. Likewise, the fly will do what the line tells it. This idea is important in getting a good drift. Check how the line is lying on the water. Remember: It controls your fly.

In the fly fishing world, making your line behave is called *mending*. Think of it as fixing or repairing your line.

What Is Mending?

Mending means adjusting your line so you get the flat drift you want.

You adjust or fix your line so your fly doesn't drag. You can do this either with a *mending cast* (adjusting to the current before the line hits the water) or by *mending your line on the water* (by picking up and adjusting some or all of the line). Often you'll be doing a little bit of both.

Mending Casts

In chapter 3, on casting, we introduced mending casts that would be useful to you: the serpentine cast and the reach cast. When you read the water and know that there will be problems with different currents pulling on the fly, you can adjust for them before the line gets to the water.

The reward for proper mending.

With the serpentine cast, instead of casting straight, you can force wavy, snakelike patterns into the line. With the reach cast, you can make your line arc to one side or another. With either cast, when your line gets on the water, it takes a while for the current to straighten out the line; therefore, your fly will float naturally a lot longer, unhampered by drag from the line. We invite you to go back to chapter 3 and review mending casts, which can save you a lot of trouble.

Another type of mending cast is the *check cast*. It's a good cast but a little more complicated. As the fly is settling on the water, you lift the rod back to the twelve o'clock position, then let the line drift straight down by lowering the rod. This is an especially good cast when delivering a fly straight downstream. A good mending cast will save you a lot of trouble. Remember the old cliché: It's better to get it right the first time.

While it's a good idea to throw a mending cast if you know you are going to have a current problem, this alone might not be enough. If you are working over a short drift, a mending cast will keep the drift drag free. If there isn't a strike, you simply take up the line and cast again. But for long drifts or for tricky water, you will also need to know how to mend your line after it's already in the water.

Mending Your Line on the Water

To keep your fly in the proper drift, you have to lift the line up before it starts to drag the fly. The most common mistake many new casters make is to wait too long to mend the drift. A fish demands that its food look natural. A fly floating on the current is a natural presentation. If the fly starts to drag, you've lost your edge. Fish spend all their lives in the water, eating from the current. They know if something looks wrong—and no fish of any size gets to be big by making a mistake like that.

Once your fly starts to drag, you've lost.

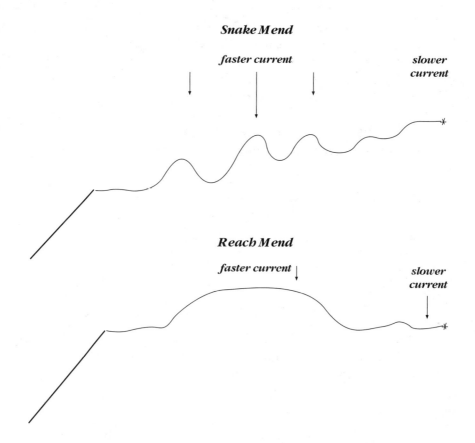

Snake Mend

faster current   slower
current

Reach Mend

faster current   slower
current

To mend without disrupting the fly, do so before the fly reaches the strike zone. Lift up on the line, taking up the slack; shake the rod tip for the snake cast; throw the body upstream for the curve cast.

Dave took this fighter because he had a natural presentation—thanks to mending.

To mend without disrupting the fly, do so before the fly reaches the strike zone. Lift up on the line, taking up the slack; shake the rod tip for the snake cast; throw the body upstream for the curve cast. Please note that this takes a lot of practice to do effortlessly.

To mend, use the rod tip to flip the line belly (the sagging part taken by the current) back upstream. Mending is almost as simple as this. Before the current has a chance to pull your line and create drag, flip it back upstream.

You'll need to be careful to not flip too hard when you mend. If you apply too much pressure, you'll either flick the fly to a new location or you'll induce the drag you were trying so hard to avoid. You want to move enough line back to keep the drift, but don't throw too much.

It takes a little bit of practice to get the right amount of mend upstream. In about fifteen minutes, you'll be mending well enough to keep a short to intermediate length of line under control. As you work with more line, it gets a little more difficult. Depending on the current, one mend might be enough. On other waters, you may need to mend half a dozen times.

A longer rod can also help because it assists you in keeping more of the line off the water. It's also easier to mend. Sometimes all you have to do is extend your arm and keep the rod high, which keeps much of the line off the water. Thus there is less line for the current to trifle with.

Good mending produces good fish. Here, Jon-Michael admires a two-and-a-half-pound brown before releasing him.

8

THE GENESIS OF FLY FISHING

The Trout

Trout are king! Or so most fly casters claim.

When you think of trout you think of fly rods. When you think of fly rods, you think of trout.

Over pizza, pasta, and apple beer, in an unassuming eatery near Gardner, Montana, a serious debate was under way among fishing friends. We were trying to agree, for the first and last time, on which trout is really the best. We wanted a definitive answer and swore not to leave until we came up with one—or until we were thrown out. The distinguished panel consisted of Casey, an advertising vice president for a large PR concern; Gary, an editor and tester at a networking corporation; Kirby, the president of a start-up high-tech company; Alan, a teacher, writer, and cinematographer; and, of course, yours truly, the trout bums Michael and Dave.

We enjoy fishing together and love the splendid game fish trout. It's our favorite subject and the topic of every conversation.

Dave is personally devoted to the brown, Gary admires the 'bow, Kirby lusts after the brookie, and Michael always chases cutthroat. Alan loves them all. Casey wisely said nothing. After a long evening of fishing tales and anecdotes, arguing over who ties the best fly or who has the tightest loops, we

A high mountain lake and a fly rod make for a lot of fun.

The trout.

came to the conclusion that all trout are wonderful and therefore equal. Perhaps Kirby said it best: "The finest trout just might be the one you have on your line."

Fighting Fish

Which fish fights the best?

No one agrees. The truth of the matter is, it depends. First of all, you have to keep the comparisons in the family. You can't compare bass to trout. A four-pound bass will nearly always feel like more fish. Look at how wide the bass is built compared to the streamlined trout. A bass sideways to you in the water is a fish that's harder to turn because there's more mass. *You have to keep the comparisons in the family.*

Even so, in-the-family comparisons don't work well, either. There are many factors in deciding among brookies, cuts, browns, and 'bows. Each species of trout will fight well or badly, depending on the conditions. Sometimes the size of the fish doesn't have much to do with it. If your experience has been like ours, you've reeled in a very good "bragging" fish and were disappointed in how it fought. It would make a good wall hanging or an excellent picture, but it was like reeling in an old army boot. Later you caught a fish that fought like Hercules; it took longer to bring in than the larger fish, and it nearly snapped your leader several times, yet it was considerably smaller.

It stands to reason that water that is well oxygenated, water that provides good food, water that is clean, and water that is near a species' ideal temperature requirement will help create a healthy fish. And a healthy fish will have a lot more spunk than an unhealthy fish. As you start to catch fish on the fringe of very hot or very cold water, you are going to find fish that are a little more stressed, fish that don't have the energy to burn on a good fight when you hook them. If the water system has been a little lean and not much has come down the conveyer belt lately, so that a fish's energy reserves aren't up to snuff, you're going to have a lethargic, hungry fish. If you catch a fish that has been stressed—perhaps it has been recently caught and released, has been chased by another predator, or is tapped out because of the spawn—you aren't going to get a good fight. And then some fish, just like some people, are stronger and more capable of putting up an effective struggle.

In ideal water, in ideal temperature, with lots of food available, any trout will put on a great show and fight like there's no tomorrow.

Now let's look at what makes trout tick.

Looking fondly at the foe.

Rainbow Trout *(Salmo gairdneri)*

The rainbow trout has a silvery look with a hint of greenish tint on its back. The color range varies. Some rainbows are quite dark, while others are almost a new-dime silver. Most have black spots scattered all over their bodies—sparsely distributed on some, generously distributed on others. Some spots are darker than others. Along the sides and gill plates are varying shades of beautiful pinks and reds (this is where the fish gets its name; it's a rainbow color). Rainbows in clear water are often distinctly marked, with colors that are vivid and stunning. Rainbow trout living in dark, stained water will have a washed-out, dull color. During the spawn, this fish (along with all trout) is most exquisite in appearance. Colors will be vivid and vibrant.

In streams, the rainbow can reach ten to fifteen pounds. In lakes, it can grow up to thirty pounds. The average fish will be 10 to 16 inches long.

The rainbow is the most beautiful trout of all!

Characteristics

Planted 'bows can be pretty dumb—but what can you expect from a fish that gets fed little green pel-

Look at the lovely lines on this 'bow.

Sometimes a Bucktail is a good way to entice a large trout.

The Serendipity is an excellent trout fly.

lets and never has to work for a living? As a result, some folks think this fish is not too smart. But consider a wild rainbow, and it's a completely different story. Here's a fish that's had to fight to stay alive, that's had to fight for its food. Here's a fish that's hard to fool. As far as being wary, a native 'bow is just a bit less bright than the brown. And a planter 'bow that manages not to be taken by a predator (human or otherwise) gets smart quickly.

Rainbow trout are the best jumpers of all the trout, noted in song and story for leaping. They are unarguably the best fighters of all the trout, particularly if they are wild fish from good water.

The rainbow is a native of the Pacific Northwest. Of all the trout, the rainbow has the widest distribution and can be found almost everywhere since it is so hearty. As a result, it's the most important trout for fisheries and anglers in general. It seems to thrive in hatcheries and takes transporting quite well.

Feeding. Rainbows feed on the standard aquatic bugs. They feed very well on the top. But above all, the 'bow is a lover of eggs, notorious for eating the eggs of all spawning fish. Egg patterns will take this stalking fish year-round. As the 'bow gets longer, it becomes more and more predatory toward other fish.

Lies. 'Bows are often in the middle of the stream. They like to lie in the riffles. They are as likely to lie in front of a rock as behind it. During the spawn, look for the rainbow below the spawning beds, where they pick up on eggs drifting in the current.

Spawning. Depending on how far north you are, the wild rainbow spawns in the spring. Occasionally, when a lot of hatchery fish have been introduced into a water system, planters will spawn any time of year. Look for gravel bars (with gravel from pea-size to silver-dollar–size) in 1 to 2 feet of water. In these areas, spawning fish will sometimes be packed as thickly as cordwood.

Ideal Temperature. 52 to 65 degrees.

German Brown Trout *(Salmo trutta)*

The German brown is an elegant fish that looks, well, some varying shade of brown. The top of the fish is deep brown to rich, dark chestnut. The bottom is lighter, a chocolate yellow. Black spots are sown over the body of this fish. Depending on the water and the location, spot size and frequency will vary and be more or less noticeable. Many fish have exquisite reddish spots with black borders. Fish in clear, cold water are usually more conclusively marked, their colors graphically apparent and striking. Browns in dark, stained water will look washed out. During the spawn, the brown (along with all trout) is most winsome, with colors bright and vivid.

In streams, the brownies can reach ten to fifteen pounds. In lakes, they can grow up to thirty pounds. The average fish is 12 to 18 inches long.

The German brown is the most beautiful trout of all!

The Muddler Minnow is a must for your fly box.

Characteristics

Brownies are the most nocturnal feeders of all trout. Because of this, some anglers presume browns are the most difficult to catch. It seems the most elusive of trout since it feeds when most fly casters aren't fishing. Successful trophy casters have learned that night is a good time to hook large trophies (and to snag your line in trees and bushes you can't see). At the very least, this extraordinary fish is more light sensitive than other trout. Morning and evening are the best times to fish for the brown. Nevertheless, a brown will fool you from time to time and feed at any time of the day the urge hits.

This fish is a native of Europe and has been called "German" brown. Our Teutonic ancestors took casting seriously. Many fly folk consider the brown the smartest of all trout. Perhaps the reason is that brown trout have been sought more aggressively than any other trout and have become wary to survive. It gets cautious quickly if there's much pressure,

This Gray Hackle Peacock is a good pattern to use when nothing else seems to work.

Releasing your fish carefully is important, but sometimes your trophy doesn't know you are trying to help it.

Elk Hair Caddis is one of the best all-around dry flies you can have in your fly box. Trout love it.

especially after it's been hooked a time or two. If you get lucky and stumble into an area that hasn't been heavily fished, you'll find these browns very naive, as gullible as cutthroats. We don't feel that the German brown is inherently smarter; it just learns faster than its cousins to avoid hooks and feathers.

Feeding. The brown is the most aggressive trout of all. It feeds heavily on anything that moves and is pugnacious toward bait fish. (And don't forget that a good hatch will bring out even the most spooky lunker.) Cautious, yes, but very assertive when feeding. This is good news for the fly caster. Fish for browns in the low light when you aren't as easily seen and when the fish is on the prowl.

Lies. German browns love seclusion. Look for undercut banks, deep holes, overhanging trees. Look for where there's shade on the water. Browns are probably the hardiest of all trout and can tolerate the warmest water. You'll often find browns in the lower reaches of a river, in water that is warmer and less oxygenated. A good example is the famous Green River in Utah and Wyoming. The farther downstream you go, the more browns you'll find.

Spawning. This lovely fish spawns in the fall. Look for gravel beds in shallow water (1 to 3 feet) with a good flow of oxygenated water. During the spawn, the male develops a kyped, or hooked, jaw. At the same time, it gets very aggressive. This is the easiest time of the year to catch a brownie.

Ideal Temperature. 52 to 68 degrees.

Cutthroat Trout *(Salmo clarki)*

The cutthroat trout is silvery with a yellowish tint. The top of the fish is a darker silver; the bottom is a lighter, yellowish color. There are black spots all over the fish; some are large, some are small. Some fish have many spots, some just a few. The spots generally become more dense toward the tail. There is usually a reddish line along the side of a cutthroat. This fish usually has a red or scarlet slash on the gill plate running under the throat and along the jaw (thus its name). In clear, cold water, cutthroats are often sharply marked, the scarlet stunning, the spots bold. Cuts living in murky, turbid water will look washed out and dull, with the scarlet bleached out and barely noticeable. During the spawn, this fish (along with all trout) is bonny. Colors will be glowing and effervescent.

In streams, the cut can reach six to ten pounds. In lakes, it can grow up to thirty pounds. The average fish will be 10 to 18 inches long.

The cutthroat is the most beautiful trout of all!

Getting ready to help net a buddy's fish. It's always exciting to watch a friend catch a good fish.

Characteristics

When you hook into a cut, you know one thing. Unlike its close cousin, the rainbow trout, this fish probably will not jump. Rainbows are jumpers, cuts aren't. If you're lucky, a fighting cut will roll on the surface, but nearly always it will dive. For this fish, depth is safety. In the meantime, this beautiful fish will give you a good strong fight while it heads deep.

The cut is a native son of the intermountain West. Waters of the Rocky Mountains and the Great Basin were originally all cutthroat habitat until other fish were introduced (as the rainbow was the fish of the West Coast). When stocking and transplanting occurred, all original ranges shifted, and those species that adapted the best remained. In many waters, the cut has a hard time competing with its close cousin the rainbow and especially with the German brown.

Very catchable is the word of the day.

Some feel the cut is the most obtuse of all trout (some think it's downright dumb). Still, it's a favorite fish among casters. True, this fish isn't as wise as the brown or as ingenious as the rainbow. But the cut is pretty (looks before brains), an alluring fish that is very vulnerable to surface flies, especially attractors.

Go fly fishing with a kid. It's a habit and a friendship that will last a couple of lifetimes.

The Scud.

Michael feels he's had the most success with white attractor patterns. Dave prefers a red or a white/red combination. We both favor terrestrials. With cutthroats, a caster can be a little sloppy with drag and presentation (although we don't recommend it since there might be a brown or a 'bow in the same water). A case in point took place on the Green River in Utah. Dave was trying one of his new beetle patterns. As a professional fly tier (that's how he helped worked his way through college), Dave is always coming up with new patterns and variations (which Michael steals when Dave's back is turned). In minutes he hooked a nice fat cut. As he was about to release his fish, it swam away with the fly.

Five hours later, about 50 yards away in a different pool, Michael caught a cut on an Elk Hair Caddis. And, yes, you guessed it. It was the same fish, still with Dave's fly in its mouth. This is amazing when you consider that there are as many as 10,000 fish per mile on the Green. The point is, cuts aren't that careful; Mike kept Dave's fly.

Feeding. Cutthroat trout feed mostly on aquatic bugs and terrestrials. Some varieties are more cannibalistic and predatory than others while some eat almost no fish at all. There are a number of subspecies, so it's hard to make sweeping generalizations. Cuts that live in lakes, where they can grow large, are often fierce predators that munch on any small fish in sight. Bear and Strawberry Lakes in Utah, Yellowstone Lake, and Pyramid Lake in Nevada are famous cutthroat waters that have hosted large fish. There is nothing a cut loves more than a good hopper or a beetle. During spawns, egg patterns will be very useful.

Lies. The cut will haunt much of the same waters as the rainbow, although they are less likely to be in front of a rock or in heavy riffles. Look for this fish at the bottom of the riffle and behind rocks that break up the flow of the current.

Spawning. This fish will spawn in the spring or early summer, depending on the water temperature and how far north it is. During the spawn, the cut, especially if it's a lake or pond fish, will move up tributaries and spawn in 1 to 2 feet of water over pea-size gravel. Often this fish will cross with its cousin, the rainbow. The result is a cut-bow.

Ideal Temperature. 52 to 65 degrees.

Brook Trout *(Salvelinus fontinalis)*

Okay!

We know the brook trout isn't really a trout. It's a char. But we'll call it a trout anyway. It's a gorgeous fish and would like to be listed with its relatives. The brookie has a slightly greenish tinge. The bottom is a dull ivory white; the flanks and fins have a maroon reddish tint with dull ivory edges. On the back of this fish are wormlike markings, separating it from the trout. The tail is square with edged, ivory borders. There are spots along the sides that have a red center with a bluish outside. Fish in spring creeks and cold streams are distinctly marked—the colors and worm marks are dazzling and attractive. During the spawn, this char (like its relative the trout) is at its prettiest.

In streams, brookies can reach up to four pounds. In lakes, they can grow up to eight pounds. The average fish will be 8 to 14 inches long.

The brook trout is the most beautiful trout of all!

Characteristics

When we think of brookies, we often think of a charming streamlined fish, not a large fish that abides in smaller waters. Some think of a fish that lives only in clean, cold streams and lakes. This native of the East Coast has been transplanted and does well in mountainous areas where the water is cold and clear. Brookies don't get as large as other trout. A three- to five-pound brookie is a large fish; a nine- or ten-pound brookie is a monster. For really

The Wooly Bugger is a good choice for big fish.

With a little practice, you can tie on a new fly in no time.

Dave takes a few minutes to match the hatch.

The Double Renegade is a good fly for lake fishing.

large brookies, about the only place left is eastern Canada.

When you hook a brookie, you're not about to get a fish that jumps out of the water like a rainbow. Instead, you get a good fighting fish that goes deep and will roll to try and spit the hook. (More than once, this maneuver has snapped the leader of a fly caster who counted the fish before it was netted.)

We feel the brookie is smarter than the cutthroat, but neither fish will ever be a rocket scientist. Like any fish, the brookie can be very gullible in low-pressure water. But in catch-and-release waters, where there is a little more fishing pressure, the brookie smartens up pretty fast. The brook trout, perhaps more than other species of trout, thrives on well-oxygenated water.

If you are fishing in the wilderness or out-of-the-way places, it may not hurt to take a mess or two of brook trout for the pan. In fact, it may help. This fish has a tendency to overpopulate and become stunted. A lot of smaller fish with large heads and small bodies will be your first clue. As a result of these traits, many western anglers don't take the brookie as seriously as they should.

Feeding. The brookie is not the surface feeder the rainbow or cutthroat is. It will come up if there is a hatch on but prefers to stay lower in the water. It likes to feed on other fish and can be very aggressive. A brook trout will take your fly with a vengeance and run like hell. For its size, it's a fighting fish.

Lies. Like the German brown, the brook trout likes the security of deep water, such as pools and back eddies. It will move out into swift water, but only to feed; then it moves back quickly. Look in the shadows and near the deep water of undercut banks. In lakes, look for underground springs and old stream channels.

Spawning. The brook char (oops, trout) spawns during the latter part of the summer in waters where winter comes quickly and during the fall in waters farther south. To spawn, the brookie heads off to graveled riffle areas (or spring-fed waters in lakes).

Ideal Temperature. 48 to 65 degrees.

Catch and Release

If you really love fish, consider releasing some of the fish you catch. As the saying goes, a fish is too valuable to catch only once. As the population of fishermen and -women grows, it stands to reason that there will be more and more catch-and-release waters. What this means is less consumption and more sport. Fishing is a pleasant way to spend your time, not simply a way to fill the freezer.

As a result of catch-and-release policies, many rivers and lakes have been brought back from poor to first-rate fishing areas. In some areas, especially in cooler waters, it takes a long time for fish to reach maturity. If too many fish are taken, it could disrupt the balance of the ecosystem.

When You Kill Fish, Consider

We're not saying you should never kill a fish or never keep a trophy for the wall. What we are saying is, think before you slam that brown in your creel. Look at the water you are fishing in. Will it hurt the system if you take a fish? Is there a lot of fishing pressure in the area? How long did it take for the fish to grow? Is the fish wild (native) or a planter?

Keep all the planters you want and let the natives go. Planted trout are often dull and pale; sometimes they have clipped or deformed fins. New planters, just dumped in the water, have not had to fight to survive. They aren't very selective. Catching a 12-inch native is a much greater accomplishment. (If a planter can survive in the water for a year, it's considered a native.)

Don't kill fish during the spawn. We can think of

It's important to carefully remove the fly and release the fish.

This fish can be caught dozens of times—handle with care!

few times when it's justified to kill a trout or bass during the spawn. This is payback time to the water system. It would be a shame to kill a fish before it had a chance to lay and fertilize eggs.

Take only enough to eat. Don't try to fill your freezer. Unless you are dealing with overpopulated panfish or are fishing during good runs of salmon or steelhead, don't bring fish back by the buckets. Fishing might have been cost-effective in the old days when you dug some worms and headed for the local pond, but it's not anymore.

When you catch the fish of a lifetime, keep it if you are going to have it mounted. Be sure you know how to take care of your trophy so it won't be wasted.

Trophy Care

Once you decide to keep that fish, you'll probably be done fishing for the day. There are a few things that you'll need to do. Taxidermists suggest you take the following steps:

- Kill the fish as quickly as possible so that it doesn't get banged up
- Don't gut the fish
- Wipe off the slime
- Put cards (or at least paper towels) under the fins
- Put paper towels under the gill covers
- Put the fish in the cooler, but keep it dry; put it on top of the ice
- Don't let the fish get wet
- Put it in a plastic bag and freeze as soon as possible
- Get the fish to your favorite taxidermist

If you take these steps, the flesh of the fish can still be eaten after the taxidermist takes what is needed. You can have both the mounted trophy and the tasty dinner.

How to Catch and Release

- *Play the fish as quickly as you can.* If the fish is worn out, it is more stressed and has a reduced chance of surviving. Remember, fighting burns up energy.
- *To land a fish faster, use a net.* Use a cotton-basket net; a nylon-basket net might be abrasive.
- *Wet your hands before grabbing the fish.* Otherwise you'll take off some of the protective slime.
- *If you can release the fly while the fish is still in the water, do so.* The less you handle the fish, the better. Sometimes you can shake the fly loose or use a hemostat with very little effort.
- *If you don't have a net, grab the fish firmly, but not too hard.* Turn the trout over on its back; this settles the fish down some. (For bass, grab by its lower lip.)
- *Use barbless hooks* (or smash down the barbs).
- *Don't horse the hook.* Use hemostats to grab the hook. This makes it much easier to grab. It's faster, too. Saving seconds during releasing saves fish.
- *If the hook is in too deeply to easily release, or too far back, cut the line.* The juices in the fish's mouth will dissolve the metal hook in a few days.
- *Make sure you are in gentle or calm water.* Never release the fish into a swift current.
- *Gently slide the fish back into the water facing the current.* Hold your hand under the fish. If it begins to swim away, let it go; it should be strong enough to swim into the gentle current. If you get fish back in the water fast, this is usually what happens.
- *If the fish is not moving much, hold your hand under the fish and gently rock it back and forth.* This is fish CPR. Hold the fish by the tail until it's strong enough to take off.

Michael released this Klamath rainbow trout—his trophy is this photo and a fine memory. He was by himself, so he placed the camera in the bow of the boat with the timer on.

Release a fish carefully so it can be caught again another day.

9

BASS, BASS, LARGEMOUTH BASS

Old Bucketmouth on a Fly

Going after largemouth bass armed with only a fly rod may be the fastest-growing aspect of fly casting. And if you've tried it, we don't have to explain why. It's great fun and a wonderful challenge. Bass will test you and your equipment, providing a great deal of sport along the way.

There's nothing like a feisty bucketmouth. This fish gets into your blood and under your skin, playing wiley games with your mind while your reel whines. A big canister-mouthed bass, as soon as he feels you set the hook line, gets smart fast. He'll head for the roughest, weediest, most structure-laden part of his territory. If you don't turn him, he's got you, and he knows it. It's his sworn duty to hook your leader up so it'll snap.

Going after immense, largemouth bass armed with only a loaded fly and bass bugs may not be a sport of kings. It just ain't genteel like spring creek trout, which sip your fly. This fellow grabs it and runs like hell. Learning what to do makes the strategy in a championship chess match look like Cub Scout amusement. You must out-think your prey or it's got you, along with an excellent bass fly and a good bit of heavy-duty leader.

While we're excellent friends, at times we get a bit competitive where bass are concerned. Nothing

Our good friend, Ken, with a fine bass.

Bass, even small ones, are fun on a fly rod.

brings this out more than fly rods, bass bags, and a patch of lily pads and cattails. It's a good thing our friends Ken or Alan are there to moderate. We can fish all day on the Green, the Madison, and the Yellowstone, the San Juan, the Beaverkill . . . no problem. We've fished hours on end, even days on end, with nice words and never the slightest hint of green envy.

But bass . . . well . . . that's a different story. It gets down and dirty, and so do we.

It's a case of blood and honor. It's a contest to the figurative fly-casting death. There's a lot of veneration in out-bassing the other guy. Each time we fish bass, which is often, we have a wager (just to make things interesting). You see, he who fishes best wins bassing honor. It goes like this: He who catches the most and he who catches the biggest.

The object is to prevail. The winner of the *most fish contest* gets to take any flies out of the other guy's box. The winner of the *biggest fish* contest gets lunch. If the same guy wins both, the *Rutter-Card Bassmasters Grand Slam to the Death,* he gets lunch, ten flies, and ten more flies. And best of all, the knowledge that the winner is the best basser of the day!

To date in the *Rutter-Card Bassmasters Grand Slam to the Death,* Dave has a slight edge on the most fish. Michael has a slight edge on the biggest fish. Next summer will be bloody.

But all in all, bass are fun. Even a dyed-in-the-wool trout person can't help but get the bass bug!

Largemouth Bass

This fish has a big mouth.

It's also the most popular sport fish in the United States. It's a very hearty, adaptive specimen. Old bucketmouth does well in a variety of areas where it has been transplanted. Bass in the twenty-pound range have been caught in waters that only recently have been stocked with this fighting game fish. If

Dave with a bass he caught near the reeds. A fly rod and a bass pond make excellent sport.

Dave is the walleye expert in the duo, Michael is the bass veteran. Say *bass* and watch him light up.

Characteristics

This bass has a big mouth because it likes to eat. And when it eats, it enjoys big bites. Large trout will be big eaters, too, but a trout is more likely to take smaller food. The body on a bass is not as streamlined or as sleek. It's designed for calm, flat waters. The bass is not a fast swimming fish like a trout. It is an ambusher. It lies behind a likely piece of structure, such as a rock or snag, and waits for its food. Then with a short burst of speed, it tries to gulp in its prey.

Because bass live in different kinds of water, the color of the fish varies. In clear water, the colors are brighter and more vivid. In darker, murky water, the color is a dull green ivory. In some waters, the fish has a fairly green appearance, and the horizontal black bar along each side is more pronounced.

To keep your dry flies floating well, use a good floatant. When you cast for bass with dries, keep them riding high in the water.

Light Sensitivity

Bass are very sensitive to light, which is one reason why they haunt fishing zones in the early and late hours of the day. Bob Underwood, in his book *Lunker,* suggests that bass are four or five times more sensitive to light than the average human being. They don't have eyelids, but they can control their pupils to regulate the amount of light that enters. They can also move their eyes forward and backward so that in dim light they can see very well. As the sun sinks, bass will move to shallower water and hang near the bottom, where they are able to see the silhouettes of food items on or near the top.

When fishing with attractor patterns, it's good to have several colors. Studies have shown that bass can discern colors fairly well. Some studies indicate that old bucketmouth might be able to see some color shades that we humans can't. Colors are important in the pattern and can sometimes make a

Dave in his kick boat, holding a nice fish. A kick boat is an excellent way to fish around the structure, required when you are casting for largemouth.

difference, although they are not a critical factor. As we've discussed with trout, the shape and size are far more important.

Like many aggressive, predatory fish, bass are a little nearsighted. This is one reason why the twitch and movement of the fly is so important. It allows the lunker to home in on the prey. A bass relies mainly on its sense of smell (which won't do the fly caster much good); most important to the caster is the fish's sense of hearing. It hears the sound of the fly as you work it through the water.

Aggressiveness

As a bass gets larger, it gets really scrappy. A bass has the same mind-set as a group of adolescent boys leaning against the school lockers, waiting to pick a fight with someone who is weak or looks different. Once a fight starts, everyone will jump in.

In the name of food, the bass will take on anything. In the name of aggression (if it's taunted or triggered), it will take on anything, only faster. Even though this fish can be very spooky, there are few things it seems to fear. Michael saw a good-size largemouth attack a perch on a stringer dangling from the bow of his canoe.

The bass is very offensive. In fact, it's downright assertive. Even if it isn't hungry, it doesn't like its private space invaded and will attack quickly. During the spawn, even the word *offensive* isn't strong enough; it's ultra-offensive. When the male is tending the nest, anything in sight gets attacked. Take advantage of this. Drift a pattern by, and you will get a strike.

Bass have a competitive quality, just like the high school boys by the lockers. It's a good thing bass aren't larger and humans smaller. We'd dare not venture into the water. Bass go into a frenzy, like sharks ripping into something. If one bass wants a fly pattern or fly, it makes the bass next door want it even more.

Temperature Requirements

When you read the water and look for structure, remember the water temperature. If the water becomes either too hot or too cold, bass get sluggish. When the water is cold, bass will be found in shallower water. When the water is warm or hot, they will be deep, except for coming up to feed. In the spring and fall, bass are in shallow water. In the summer, they stay deeper but come up to eat. Adjust your fishing to where the fish are.

Bass have a pretty wide temperature zone, from about thirty-five to ninety degrees Fahrenheit. They seem to enjoy water in the seventies the best. (They will feed very actively in water up to eighty-four degrees.)

Fishing Methods

When fishing for bass, you are trying to entice, or trigger, the fish's response. It will take your pattern because it looks good or because it provokes its aggressive instincts. If something looks tempting to eat, perhaps your pattern, it will trigger a hunger-feeding response. The way you work the fly will trigger either a hunger or an aggression response.

Always keep in mind that bass are bullies to the core and love to pick on whatever looks weak and struggling. Competition is another trigger. If one fish wants it, another fish will want it more.

Michael was using a frog pattern on a backwater bayou in east Texas when he cast by a likely snag near an undercut bank. A medium-size bass shot out of nowhere and missed the pattern (or else Michael set the hook too soon and pulled it out of the fish's mouth). During the commotion, he moved his frog about a yard. After the miss he let it sit. Then he twitched it a little. He let it sit again, then he thrashed it about. This time, two bucketmouths shot after the lure, both coming out of the water and making a mighty splash, each trying to beat the other out of the froggy meal.

Michael releases a fish he caught in a deep pond on the Utah desert. When the water temperature near the surface warms, many fish seek the cool depths.

The hopper is an excellent bass offering.

The battle made the fish want Michael's pattern more. He finally caught both fish—then another within 6 feet of the log. All the thrashing on the water seemed to serve as a dinner bell to other largemouth. The competitiveness made the fish less wary and more aggressive.

If you've fished with live bait for bass, you'll understand. You've probably noticed several fish fighting for the same bite, at times even trying to take what's left of the minnow from the bass that's hooked. For this reason, it's not a bad strategy to cast back to water where you've failed to set the hook after a strike or caught a fish.

With trout, once you've hooked a fish, you often have dead water for a while. The thrashing and movement spook wary trout. But, all this activity only excites bass. If all you are catching is small bass, you might just continue fishing in the same spot and let the youngsters thrash about all they want. More than one good bass caster has used this method to excite the interest of the big brothers in the area. Here's an example of what we are talking about:

One of Michael's friends, who lives near Lake Berryessa, just north of San Francisco, was having a picnic in a cove with his family. Not being one for waterskiing, he kept an eye on the kids while his wife took a few turns about the lake on her new slalom ski. Never being far from a fly rod, he put the baby to sleep, assembled his four-piece rod, and tied on a bright orange popper. He waded into the water and started fishing near a large rock and dead tree that had partly fallen in the water.

He couldn't go out more than a few yards since he needed to keep an eye on the baby, so he cast to the structure and worked the popper. Before long he was catching his share of small bass. Even small largemouth bass were better than no bass—and he couldn't move anyway—so he kept at it. Later, he hooked a larger fish. Before the boat came back, he had hooked several nice fish. He feels that the feeding commotion the younger bass caused created a competitive mood that triggered something aggressive in the larger fish, which is why they came in for a look (and a hook).

Location

The first question to ask when you set out to catch bass is: Where are the fish? You can't catch the fish if you can't find them.

Bass are fickle critters, and they move about. It's hard to pin them down. The range of a bass is extensive, so any generalization won't be true all the time. At Lake Powell, not far from where we live, I've seen and caught bass in 40 to 50 feet of clear, cool water. In the east Texas swamp referred to earlier, the average depth might be 5 to 10 feet and the water murky and warm. This is a very versatile fish. Talk to locals who are familiar with an area. Ask them if the bass are usually in one area during one time of the year and in another later on. Consult books, local magazines, tackle shops, sporting goods stores, boat shops, and state fish and game folks: All are good sources. At least they'll get you pointed toward the right side of the lake, swamp, river, or pond. After that, it's up to you.

Structure

Structure—that is, objects in the water—is critical when it comes to bass. Find the structure, and you'll find the bass.

Bass use structure for waiting in ambush. Think like the bass. Where would you hide? Look for old bigmouth near snags, by rocks, in the shadows, in weeds, on the shady side of weeds, near moss, under docks, or on a ledge.

Look for places bass can hide and still see to ambush a meal. If you've ever watched bass in clear water, you'll know they seem to come out of nowhere and take the pattern hard. They can blend into the scene quite well. If you don't have polarized glasses, you'll be at a great disadvantage. A hat with a brim helps, too.

The Matuka is an excellent bass pattern. It looks like a tempting minnow flitting about.

This bass was caught in 6 inches of water under a willow tree.

Time of day is another consideration. In the summer, especially if it's very hot, you'll want to fish at night (if that's legal) or in the evening and early morning. The warm water will be uncomfortable for the bass, and coming into a feeding zone during the heat of the day will be too much. You'll have to ambush the fish while they are coming in to ambush prey. Since you've identified their structure, you'll know where to cast flies.

Movement

Work the wet flies off the bottom and make that pattern dance. Move it past the likely area in the structure. You must give life to a bass fly. Nearly always, you as the caster give it the action. Make the pattern look like a living meal. You don't need to be delicate or coy. Be bold.

For surface flies, often referred to as *poppers,* don't worry about a delicate, soft-as-snow presentation. *Drop that sucker down so it plops!* In the first place, a bass likes to see its food. There's no current to carry it to the fish; the fish goes to it. A plop is like a dinner bell. A bass also likes to see a little movement and some struggling. After you drop that fly, make it look alive or slightly injured. Move that pattern about. Maybe make it skip across the water, make it twitch.

If this doesn't do the trick, pick up the fly and drop it again. You may get the bass to take another look.

We were fishing gravel pits one summer. The morning was quite good. We had caught a number of good fish. Then everything seemed to die out at once. For more than an hour, there was hardly a rise. Then Michael tied on a couple of hoppers. "Flog the water by those reeds," he suggested. "There's quite a few hoppers, and they're making a plop. Let's make some really big splashes. Don't have anything else to lose."

To make a long story short, Dave snuck up through the oozing mud until he was 30 feet from the reeds. He slapped the water as hard as he could. It must have excited the bass; for the next several hours we worked our way around the banks of the pond, picking up a good number of fish. We couldn't slap the water hard enough.

Tackle

Any equipment you have will work on bass, but some types of gear will work better than others. With bass, you'll need a stiffer rod.

Rods. A largemouth bass is a big-bodied fish that can be hard to turn in the water. Also, since you are fishing in waters that have a lot of structure, and thus a lot of potential snags, you need a rod that allows you to horse your fly if it's hung up. A sensitive #5 or #6 rod could easily be compromised with too much pressure. And lastly, you'll be throwing bigger and heavier flies. You need a rod that can do it adequately.

A #7 or #8 rod would be our choice for largemouth bass. In some waters, even a #9 rod might be the right choice. Most casters use an 8-foot to 9-foot rod. We lean more toward the long rod length.

Lines/Leaders. By all means, a weight-forward (WF) line is the best choice. A double-taper line is adequate, but it doesn't have the advantages of a WF line. The WF line will cast farther (delicacy isn't critical here), and it will turn larger flies more easily. Your leader must be a little stiffer, perhaps a 1X. The average length would be 7½ to 9 feet (you might go shorter if you're using a wet fly).

Flies. Most of the flies you use will be from #2 to #6. For wet bass flies, your first choice would be large flies that imitate bait fish, frogs, leeches, polliwogs, hoppers, crickets, and crayfish. Dave is very partial to a Muddler Minnow. Michael likes the leech pattern best. There are a great many variations in bass flies. Just like smallmouth-bass patterns, these flies can be divided into surface flies, poppers (which splash and pop on the film), streamers

Bass are a little more hearty than trout. Nevertheless, they still have to be released with care.

(which dive), and others (which loosely fit into all categories). You might consider the following flies for your box:

- Poppers #1/0 to #8
- Marabou Leech (green, black, white, red) #1 to #8
- Crayfish #1/0 to #6
- Muddler Minnow #1/0 to #10
- Hopper (Joe's is a good choice) #2 to #10
- Zug Bug #8 to #14
- Marabou Muddler Minnow #6 to #8
- Bucktail Streamers (any color) #2 to #10
- Sculpin Minnow #1/0 to #6
- Frog #2 to #6

When fishing, keep your eye on the pattern and get ready to set the hook up to the last moment. A bass will often wait, following the pattern, to the last possible second before attacking.

A small bug might be the perfect thing for a two-pound trout, but a two-pound bass wants a little more. It wants a big bite. Bass do feed on bugs, and bug patterns can be useful, but it's usually the larger insects that tempt this fish. Also, they attack other fish. A big bite to a bass, if it has a choice, is a small fish, not a caddis. Generally, patterns need to be bigger and more visible than when you're fishing for trout.

10

WARM-WATER FIGHTERS

Fighting Fish on a Fly

First, we'd better say that the term "warm water" is somewhat misleading.

As a generalization, we've lumped a lot of fish in this category. But it's not completely accurate. Yes, most of these fish do well in warm water (probably better than trout), yet it's not out of the ordinary to find a "warm-water" fish in cool water.

For example, within miles of our homes, there is a trophy population of brown trout, walleye, and white bass. A nearby reservoir boasts good numbers of rainbow and brown trout, walleye, largemouth bass, and perch. Local spring-fed farm ponds hold large bass and lunker trout, and reservoirs contain northern pike, trout, walleye, and bass. A little farther away, the Flaming Gorge boasts world-record brown trout, is famous for its giant lake trout, and has a fantastic population of smallmouth bass.

You see our point? But until we can get another word into the fishing magazines and books, "warm water" will have to do, even if the water in question isn't always all that warm.

Dave with a striper he caught on a fly rod at Lake Powell. It's a nice mount for his den.

Why Warm-Water Fish on a Fly?

First of all, it's a lot of fun, and why limit the fun? You can't get enough.

Another reason is that you don't have to have a delicate presentation. In fact, a loud slap when you hit the water is often to your advantage. Go ahead, let that line crash into the water. Let that popper, streamer, or whatever pattern you're using slam on the film. This is a style of fishing where a clumsy cast can work for you. Work on your casting style, but still catch a lot of fish while you're at it.

Fishing for warm-water species has been gaining in popularity over the past few decades. This ruffles the feathers of the fly-casting purist, but that's too dang bad. It's true that the delicate techniques and stylized approaches used when casting for trout aren't essential when throwing flies for warm-water fish. On the other hand, anyone who's used a fly rod to lure a wily ol' pike out from under its lily pad, hooked a round-bellied crappie on a marabou streamer, danced a Matuka in front of a cunning walleye, or fought a feisty smallmouth will agree: Warm-water fish are a lot of fun and a great challenge for the fly caster.

It's not mindless "toss that pattern," either, as some would have you believe. Sure, the cast is less delicate, but there are a lot of other skills involved. We would suggest that warm-water fish are worthy opponents for fly casters any way you look at it.

At times, certain populations of warm-water fish, such as bluegill, perch, and crappie, are very easy to catch. Many times such panfish are in desperate need of a good "thinning." Where you might feel guilty taking a big mess of brown trout out of a stream, you'll be encouraged to take a bucketful of bluegill, perch, or crappie home for the frying pan. Many argue that panfish are the best eating, too.

Another advantage is location. Many anglers have to travel to get to their favorite trout stream. Such a trout-casting trip may not be possible without a lot of planning and time off. Often, trout don't do well near people, development, and agriculture. But, there are probably places right under your nose where you can cast a fly for a great "warm-water" game species.

Yes, we're dyed-in-the-wool trout casters. But it's possible to love and worship trout as well as love and worship smallmouth bass and crappie at the same time. It's no accident that we live in the heart of the best trout fishing in the world, and it's no surprise that we usually fish for trout. Nevertheless, a dozen times a year, in addition to many local trips, we're liable to load up and drive to whatever water looks good. Even if it's a thousand miles away.

As a point of interest, Dave is just a few ounces shy of breaking the Utah state walleye record. How's that for a blue-blooded trout caster? Michael is green with envy.

Speaking at a fishing seminar, on the subject of crossover casting, Michael said he loved chocolate. "Yet, in spite of my love, I've never turned down a sugar cookie or a ginger snap. I love cookies. Just because I love chocolate, however, it doesn't mean I'd turn down another treat, too."

To emphasize his point, he stuffed a Snickers bar in his mouth. Then he pulled a package of sugar cookies out of his knapsack and started eating them. He continued the lecture after he shared his cookies.

We recommend a lot of crossover casting if the opportunity presents itself.

Why?

Because a predator is a predator! And why limit yourself to one kind of fish or fishing? Sure, you'll have your favorites, but variety is the spice of life. There are more common elements than differences. If you know trout, you know more about bass than you might at first realize. Fish are fish, and while some of the numbers might change, they all like to live in their comfort zone. Fish need a source of food, a place to rest, and protection from larger predators. Reading the water is still reading the water and entomology is still entomology. Many of the suggestions we've made about trout can be directly transferred over to warm-water fish.

A smallmouth bass caught on a Wooly Bugger.

Smallmouth Bass

As far as we're concerned, this is *the* fly caster's warm-water fish. The smallmouth bass started out mostly as a river fish. It has been stocked and transplanted, but it doesn't take as readily to new waters as the largemouth. One reason is that it can't stand as much direct competition as other species of fish. North-central to northeastern Canada, the upper Mississippi, and the Tennessee and Ohio drainages are the smallmouth strongholds. In other regions, the smallmouth thrive in isolated locations.

Even if you aren't in the heartland of the smallmouth, check your local area. Good smallmouth fishing might be nearer than you think. In our part of the world, Flaming Gorge Reservoir is a smallmouth paradise, and I've had plenty of great days hauling in tons of fish.

The Fighter

For many anglers' sporting dollar, the smallmouth bass is the most fightin' of all the game fish. As Michael summed it up in an article, "The smallmouth is a package of dynamite." This fly-shaking, leader-stretching, nerve-wracking, marriage-breaking fish is an addiction. The smallie doesn't have the draw that the largemouth has, partly due to more limited distribution, but once you cast a few flies and get the bug, you'll be a true-blue convert.

This little air jumper doesn't get as big as its big-mouthed cousin, but talk about fight! The largest smallmouth that we know about topped the scales at just under twelve pounds. It was nearly 27 inches long and had a girth of nearly 22 inches. This little hummer was caught on Dale Hollow Lake in Kentucky. What a fish!

Most of the smallmouth that we mere mortals catch weigh from two to three pounds. Once in a while, we'll hook into one that pushes four or five pounds. But you have to know that bigger ones are out there waiting for your perfect presentation.

Not long ago at Flaming Gorge, Michael did battle with a fish so feisty and mean that our fishing buddies put their money on the fish and not on Mike. He was in a float tube working some structure off a point. Our buddies were eating lunch, trying to decide whether to throw rocks at Michael or to get in their float tubes and join the quest for the perfect smallmouth.

Michael was fishing a light #3 rod with a small leech. He had changed to a light tippet to give the pattern more life in the water and to "give the fish a sporting chance." He gave a loud howl as he saw his rod tip go down. For the next five minutes Dave watched a smallmouth actually pull Michael about the cove. With such a light leader and a very sporting rod, the fish had its way. After the little fighter was worn out enough to get in close, Michael reached for the fish. Wrong move. It took off again, doing an air walk and a couple of sounding dives. The fish fought its heart out. Finally, Michael reeled in his smallmouth and held it up. It was the biggest fish any of us had seen on that water, and the biggest smallmouth Michael had ever caught. He unhooked the exhausted fish and carefully released it back into the water.

The folks on shore were clapping. It was a marvelous show, much better than the fishing battles on Saturday morning TV. Michael thought they were clapping for him. Actually, they were applauding the heart and spirit of such a fighting fish. That fish is still swimming in Flaming Gorge.

A beetle pattern is an excellent fly in late summer.

Smallmouth love to hold on the edges in early spring.

Characteristics

The term *smallmouth* is a little misleading. Yes, this fish has a small mouth compared to the largemouth, but the mouth ain't that small.

The way to tell a smallmouth from a largemouth is first by looking at the fish's eye. Draw a pretend line straight down. If the jaw extends beyond the eye, it's a largemouth. If it doesn't, it's a smallmouth.

Also, there is no horizontal black bar along the side. In smallmouth bass, the eyes are very large, there are dim spots on the sides of the body, and the caudal fin is yellow.

As this fish grows older, it takes on a more greenish gold bronze color. The intensity of the color varies with water clarity and temperature. In more stained water, a smallmouth fish will be less green-tinted and a little more bronze yellow.

As a rule, smallmouth bass like cooler water. Their ideal temperature range is sixty-four to seventy-six degrees. They don't like competition, so if necessary, they can push their optimum temperature zone without ill effects. The hearty smallie can function well in warm water if it has to, and in cool water, too. Instead of competing, it will move to less productive areas.

Like most fish, the smallmouth bass is an opportunistic fish. If something looks good, no matter when or where, there is a chance that it will take it. This is very good news for the fly caster. Anytime can be feeding time. Sometimes, as with trout, this fish can be selective. And then at other times you can take them on a bare hook. As a general rule, this fish is very catchable but can be challenging.

Depending on the body of water and the opportunity, a smallmouth bass will eat crayfish, hellgrammites, sculpin, waterdogs, frogs, rough fry (shiners, smelt, perch, char), game fry, mayflies, caddis flies, stone flies, damsels, dragonflies, and a host of other things. The smallmouth and the trout have a lot of similarities.

Fishing Methods

If you can, fish around something. It's not very often you'll find smallmouth bass "just out there."

Structure

Yes, this is a structure-oriented fish. Notwithstanding competition from other fish and changes in temperature, the smallmouth will always move toward physical objects and shadows in the water. In rivers, streams, and lakes, look for cracks in rocks, outcropping branches, and logs. Look for a rock face that has corners and angles extending into the water or a slide of rocks that extends into the water. Look for other kinds of structure, such as a moss bank or a place where stained and clear water meet.

While clear water might be more aesthetically pleasing, dirty water might make for better fishing. On Flaming Gorge, a good way to fish smallies is to follow the wind. As the chop picks up in the afternoon, waves hitting the shallow areas make it rather silty. Smallmouth bass follow the silt in and feed in several feet of water. Look for muddy water.

If the water is clear, you'll have to go deeper.

Fishing in Rivers

Most folks seem to concentrate on lakes more than rivers because a lake is relatively static and a little easier to predict. But there are reasons to try smallmouth fishing in rivers. What you have learned about trout fishing will carry over and pay smallmouth dividends here. Smallmouth bass in streams are usually less selective; they'll eat almost anything you throw at them if it's presented right. Another plus is that the rivers might be less crowded with people who are fishing.

The major thing to remember is the current itself. It is the element that makes lake and river fishing so different. What we have discussed earlier in this book about reading water and stalking trout holds true for smallmouth bass. Remember, there are a lot of similarities between the two fish. A river is a dynamic environment, always changing. Ask yourself what the fish needs to meet its requirements for food, shelter, and comfort.

Always keep structure in mind. In this case, how does the structure break up the current? Where can the smallmouth hide or escape from the current and still feed? Remember that fish in streams require a lot

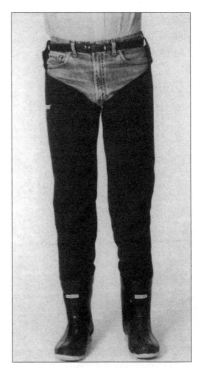

Hip waders, at the least, are a must for river fishing.

more to eat because of the energy they burn just staying "current" with the current. Where is the fish safe? They want protection from below, but mostly need it from above. Smallmouth, like rainbow trout, tend to favor waters that are somewhat fast.

Don't worry too much about the strike zone or the perfect drift. A cast right on the nose is about the right place. As an aside, nymphs can be effective if you dead drift them right in front of the fish. (If you're used to top-water action such as a dramatic take, however, you won't get it using a nymph. The take is very subtle, and you have to really watch to set the hook.)

Start your fishing around areas that break the flow of the current. A key to success with smallmouth (as with trout) is understanding what is going on at the bottom as well as what is going on at the top.

It's important to work the fly with these fish. If you've fished the flies known as streamers, you will have the advantage. Work the fly in a progressive pattern. Let the pattern stop, then pick it up again. Study the casts we suggest for the wet and dry fly in the next two chapters. These casts work very well for smallmouth on rivers, and you need not cast delicately as you would for trout. Some of our favorite stream flies are hellgrammites, stone flies, hoppers, and large nymphs.

Fishing in Lakes

When you are fishing wet on a large body of water, you must put the life into the fly. A sinking line, such as a Scientific Anglers Stillwater or Uniform Sink Plus One is a good option. This will take the belly out of your line and thus speed up response time. You have to keep up your level of concentration, however, or you'll miss the pickup. Depending on the water, fish your sculpin, minnow, and leech patterns on the bottom. If they aren't weighted, add some shot. Matukas are good patterns, too, because of the dorsal-fin silhouette they project in the water.

The wooly worm and marabou leech are great patterns, and they are versatile. Experiment with your retrieve. These patterns can be taken for minnows, aquatic insects, or crayfish. Start by fishing in 3-inch strips, then letting it sit.

Smallmouth are very fond of crayfish. Crayfish like rocks, and bass will gather in rocky areas to feed. Such a disturbance dislodges crayfish and attracts more fish. Michael has caught more than forty fish in two hours under such conditions.

On those days when it all comes together and the bass are taking off the top water, it's more than great to be alive. The action starts in the spring and usually ends sometime in early fall. Throw out your popper and go to work. (Remember to keep your popper dry so it will pop and dance on the water.) You'll love the way they take the fly off the top of the water.

Cast your fly and let it sit. Then give it a twitch or two. Let it sit. Then snap it a time or two. Let it sit. Twitch it again. Let it sit. Then snap it. Experiment with other retrieves.

We picked up a number of bass with a Parachute Hare's Ear.

Tackle

Rods. Most books will tell you to start with a #6 rod. We won't argue except to say that a smallmouth on a #5 is one of life's sheer joys. (Perhaps a #5 rod is too small for streams, even though that's all we use for smallies.) A #5 to #7 is about the right rod for the job.

Lines/Leaders. A floating line is the first choice in weight forward or bass taper, although a double taper will do. Leaders will be 4X to 2X in 9-foot lengths. Depending on conditions, the leader/tippet requirements will vary. In clear waters you might need to tie on a fine, long leader. When you fish wet, you'll want to shorten up the leader.

A Deer Hair Popper.

Flies. Almost any fly that works for a largemouth bass will work for a smallmouth if it is downsized a little. Almost any fly that works for a trout, with the exception of some of the very small flies, will work for a smallmouth. If given a choice, the smallmouth bass, like the largemouth, will take a big bite. There are many variations of patterns. You'll need several in various sizes and colors. Just like largemouth patterns, these flies can be divided into surface flies, poppers (which splash and pop on the film), streamers (which dive), and others. Consider the following flies for your tackle box:

- Deer Hair Poppers #2 to #8
- Hellgrammite Nymph #4 to #10
- Marabou Leech (green, black, red, white) #2 to #12
- Hoppers #2 to #14
- Crayfish #1 to #4
- Muddler Minnows #1/0 to 8
- Zug Bug #8 to #14
- Marabou Minnow #6 to #8
- Bucktail Streamers (any color) #2 to #10

Poppers will range in size from #1/0 up to #8. A range of #2 to #4 has been the most productive for us. Dave likes the ones with rubber legs. Michael likes the streamlined ones best. Deer hair and marabou are the most common popper materials, although we have tied a successful pattern with moose hair. While you are filling your box, also consider dragonfly patterns, wooly worm patterns, sculpins, and zonkers.

As we suggested with largemouth bass, keep your concentration up as you fish. Don't let your mind drift. Be ready to set the hook up to the last moment. A smallmouth bass will often wait, following the pattern, until the last possible moment before attacking. Perhaps it's playing cat-and-mouse with its food. Many good fish are caught within feet of the shore, the boat, or the caster.

Striped Bass

Maybe stripers are the strongest fighters of all the freshwater fish. Maybe even stronger than small-mouth bass.

"Boys," the old man at the marina gas station shouted, "ya cain't catch them striped bass with fly rods. Don't ya know nothing a-tall!"

With a full tank we continued up the road, eyes peeled on the water known as Lake Powell. "Stop." Dave looked through field glasses.

"This is the place." An ecstasy of fumbling as we unloaded and headed for the blue water.

Michael hit the gas on the small motor, and the Porte-Boat moved out into the channel. The man at the gas station would have a fit if he really knew. Yes, you can catch striped bass on a fly rod when conditions are right, and it's a whole lot of fun. On Dave's #9 and Michael's #8, we landed striper after striper. Some went almost twenty pounds. The leader broke when Michael carelessly netted Dave's best fish; he went in after the fish, with a push from Dave, to atone for his carelessness.

Stripers are found in open waters and in some river systems. They often are a deep-water fish, and when they're down, it's hard to catch them using a fly rod. But aggressive predators like stripers have to eat. They eagerly follow the schools of shad and will come up to shallow water to feed. This is the time they are the most available to the fly rodder.

While we won't go into detail on this fish, because its availability is somewhat limited, let us suggest you try fishing for it if the opportunity presents itself.

You need something that floats for this type of fishing: a float tube, a canoe, a boat. Michael likes a folding boat like the Porte-Boat, which fits nicely on top of a car. When we see signs of striped bass—birds going after the shad that attract stripers, or "boiling" water where masses of stripers are

A portable boat is a good way to seriously fish bass waters.

feeding—we unload the light little boat, grab our vests and rods, and race for the water. Stripers follow schools of bait fish and will gorge themselves in hysterical feeding frenzies. This often occurs under ledges and at the edges of structure.

You need a fairly heavy rod, #8 to #9. A floating and a sinking line with lots of backing and an adventurous attitude are also necessary. For flies, use large poppers and large (#1/0 to 4), weighted streamers (yellow, white, black). Use a leader that has at least a six-pound test. If you are throwing a weighted fly, a 9-foot piece of mono line will work. This isn't fancy fishing.

Sometimes the stripers are right on the surface, tearing into tender shad. If this is the case, tie on a popper and cast to the boil. Cast as far and as fast as you can. Then strip your fly back as fast as you can. You can even hold the rod under your elbow and strip the line with both hands. You can't pull it in fast enough. The faster you pull it, the more it triggers an aggressive response in the stripers, who have visions of a fleeing fish or a wounded fish.

If you can see the boil but no stripers on the top, tie on a weighted pattern and cast over the boil. Wait until the pattern sinks. Then strip it back for all you're worth.

When you get a striper on, it'll test your mettle. It's not unusual to have the striper rip your fly to shreds.

Bluegill

It's not a cliché, it's a fact of life: You can't get enough of a good thing.

It was a hot summer, and except in the high mountains, the trout had shut down on our favorite waters. Yes, we were still catching fish, but it was tough.

"It's been a while since we've been 'gilling," Dave said.

"Good idea!" Michael responded coldly. It took

Michael about a year to get back into the bluegill game. The last time we had a bluegill trip, Michael got a little careless and let one of the combating little buggers run his stiff spine through the float tube. He got stranded on the marshes of Utah Lake and had to walk back to his car the long way carrying a half-dead Browning float tube.

With no further thought on Dave's part, and a hint of fear on Michael's, we headed off to some ponds everyone else, except for a few smart farm kids, always seemed to pass up near town. Like a couple of country boys (which we are), we started 'gilling.

After a few casts, Dave landed a bluegill that went about a pound—a good fish by 'gill standards. After a few casts Michael forgot about the 'gill that sunk his ship and was catching fish, too.

Going after bluegills is refreshing. A lot of folks relegate this little fighter into the realm of "boy's" fish. When you grow older you graduate to bigger and better-finned adventure, leaving bluegill behind like patched-kneed blue jeans. And yet, while at times bluegill are easy to catch, we discovered there is a minor art to consistently hooking them.

Bluegill are easiest to catch in the spring during the spawn. At this time of the year, they are easiest to find. They take about everything you throw at them, and they practically fall into your net. However, with a little practice, bluegill can be caught all year, and they're fun for adults, too.

The best place to focus your search for bluegill is coves where the water isn't too deep and near the mouths of streams. (Usually stream water is warmer, plus it carries a lot of food for the waiting fish.) If you can, wade out so you are casting parallel to the shore. You'll get a much better action on your fly.

In the spring, use a weighted #8 to #10 Wooly Bugger in black or green. You'll have to play with the action to see what these little fighters like at the time. During the summer, bluegills go deeper to get to more comfortable water. During these times, it's usually best to fish in the early morning and later evening.

Look for structure, docks, old logs, rocks, car bodies, or moss lines. If it's really hot, don't overlook weed banks. In the summer when the heat has depleted the oxygen from the water, weeds not only offer shade and protection from the sun, they absorb carbon dioxide from the water and provide better oxygenation.

Use a #12 to #14 Wooly Bugger in black, green, or white as your wet fly of choice. Bluegill feast on terrestrials as summer wears on. Cricket and hopper patterns are good choices; so are flies with rubbery legs. Try #12 to #16 dries.

While poppers can be deadly any time of the year, the later summer and early fall may be the best time to try them. If one method doesn't work, try another. The key to catching lots of fish is experimentation. Bluegill are excellent fare. Taking out a mess of fish is often good for the water.

Panfish

There's a reason panfish are called *panfish*. They fit so nicely in a pan. Another advantage to this little treasure is that they reproduce so fast there's often little harm in taking a large batch home for an old-fashioned fish fry. Panfish—crappies, perch—are hearty little fighters that turn a day with a fly rod into a day of fun. It's true that a fish of this persuasion isn't likely to break your rod, but it *is* fun fishing.

These fish are fighters, but they're also predators. Everything we've discussed about reading water, and especially structure, is applicable. You'll want to look for hiding places—weed beds, shelves, snags, docks, old cars, tires. It's a joy to take a panfish off the surface; enjoy it when it happens. Most of the time, however, you'll need to fish wet flies. Use the same type of retrieves we discussed with smallmouth and largemouth bass.

Depending on the time of year, these little warm-water fish will be shallow or deep. The warmer the weather, the deeper they go. Remember, they are lower on the food chain than bass, so someone is always after them. Ask yourself where you would hide in the water if you were a panfish.

Because these fish are smaller, with smaller mouths, you'll need to use a smaller hook and pattern. This is also a good time to break out a smaller rod, a #3 on up. The lighter the rod, the more action you'll feel. Your presentation need not be delicate. A good solid plop on the water is a good calling card.

When you work the fly, you don't need to put quite as much action in it as you would for bass. Start off your day with twitches and coy movements. If this doesn't work, start toward more aggressive strips and motions.

Favorite flies for crappie/perch (mostly wet flies, since neither fish comes to the surface that often):

- Wooly Worm (black and green) #8 to #14
- Deer Hair Popper #6 to #12
- Wooly Bugger (black, white, green) #6 to #12
- Black Gant (wet) #10 to #16
- Marabou Leech (black, green, red, white) #4 to #14
- Bucktail Wing #6 to #14

Favorite flies for bluegill:

- Wooly Worm (black and green) #8 to #14
- Golden Ribbed Hare's Ear #12 to #18
- Deer Hair Popper #6 to #12
- Black Gant (wet) #10 to #16
- Sponge Fly #8 to #12
- Ants #10 to #14

Walleye

This elusive fish is not a great fish to attack with a fly rod, but it can be done. Walleye are predators, and they eat other fish. Any minnow patterns are effective.

This is a mount of Dave's almost-record-breaking walleye. It missed the Utah state record by four ounces. He caught it on a #6 rod.

For smaller fish in the one- to two-pound range, when they move into streams, you can be successful if you dead drift nymph patterns with the current. The pickup is soft, so be ready to set the hook.

The best time to take them is during the spawn, when they come into shallow waters. Favorite waters are feeder streams. At times, larger fish seem to prefer a more lively retrieve. At other times they seem to want a slow twitch. There are no set rules with walleye. Experiment with your retrieve.

Favorite walleye patterns:

- Wooly Bugger (all colors) #1/0 to 4
- Zonkers #1/0 to 4
- Matukas #1/0 to 4
- Marabou Leech #1/0 to 8

11

GOING DOWN AND DEEP

Fishing the Wet Fly

Wet-fly casting is the oldest form of fly fishing. Historians of fly fishing have traced the wet feathered hook back thousands of years. And contrary to some very snobbish dry-fly casters, it's not a lower form of fly fishing. You'll probably enjoy more initial fishing success with a wet fly, yet you won't learn it all overnight. You can push your wet-fly technique as far as you dare and still have more to learn.

Let's review. What is wet-fly fishing and what's a wet fly?

Wet-fly fishing is determined mostly by *manner,* not always by the actual fly itself. In other words, *how* you're fishing the fly is the determining factor. If you're fishing underwater, you're wet-fly fishing.

Hooking a trout that dry-fly casters had overlooked.

There are some basic differences between wet and dry flies, but there is also a fair amount of crossover. Nevertheless, in a generic sort of way, on many wet flies, the hackles are soft (coming from hens instead of roosters). This helps the fly look more alive in the water. The wings are often tied so they lie back. The hook is generally longer and heavier.

Wet-fly fishing is not as casting-intensive as dry-fly fishing. You can make mistakes without scaring fish.

Sometimes you have to weight your fly to get it to the fish. Notice the twist of lead several inches above the head of the pattern.

Fishing a wet fly, at least on the primary level, isn't as difficult as throwing dry flies. When you cast dries, you have to be exacting. Because the fish are near the surface, you have to cast so the line doesn't hit the water or drop down too near a feeding fish. Most of your dry-fly fishing effort is spent getting the cast right. The margin for error is rather narrow. One mistake and the fish are gone, and you need to move to another section of the stream.

If you cast poorly or slap the water while fishing wet flies, however, you're not likely to scare the fish. They're probably too deep to know you're still learning the finer points of this sport. And while you sometimes have to pay attention to drag with different styles of wet casting, it isn't as critical as it is when you are throwing dry flies. You'll be doing more fishing and less worrying about casting.

Because the fish you're after are in deep water, they feel safe and aren't as apprehensive as they would be on or near the surface. Since they feel assured, they will feed more naturally and are less likely to be temperamental or to demand a specific food.

You'll want to match the food they're eating as closely as you can, but you don't need to worry about being so specific. You can get away with a more general, impressionistic pattern.

About 80 to 90 percent of the time, fish feed under the film. This is why a wet-fly caster can nearly always be successful.

As a wet-fly caster, you'll be throwing a number of pattern flies. Fish under the film feed on small fish; aquatic bugs, from nymphs to emergers to larvae; waterlogged terrestrials; crustaceans like crayfish and scuds (shrimp); and frogs; snakes; and tadpoles. Wet-fly patterns that are more specific will be somewhat neutral in color—browns, grays, blacks. *A general rule of thumb: When in doubt, try to match the color on the bottom of the river or lake.* Much of the aquatic life has evolved to that color for protection. For attractor patterns, the colors might be more flashy and bright.

In this chapter we'll discuss how to get set up to fish flies wet, explain some basic wet-fly fishing strategies and casts, and talk about how to fish various types of wet flies.

How to Get Set Up

While some casters get really technical about this, you don't need any fancy gear.

Rod. Your regular trusty rod will probably do. Since you'll be throwing some weight when you cast wets, the minimum size rod will probably be a #5. Most wet fishing is done on a #5 or #6 rod. Unless we're casting in large bodies of water, or are after big fish, we both prefer a light rod. With a light rod you get excellent fishing action, but you have to be a little more careful when you cast the heavier flies. And you can't cast as far as with the heavier rods. A heavy rod gives you a little more power when you are trying to turn over a heavier fish. It's also easier to roll cast and set the hook.

Reel and Line. Your regular reel will work just fine. So will your regular fly line. In some waters, especially deep water, a sinking line or a sinking tip line might be an advantage—but don't worry about that for now. In the meantime, use what you've got, and you'll be successful. About 80 percent of wet-fly fishing is done with a floating line.

Leader. You can use your regular leaders. In many situations, however, you'll want to clip them down and make them shorter. When you are fishing streamers (heavy flies), perhaps you'll go as short as 3 to 4 feet with a sinking line or 9 feet with a floating line. On nymphs and emergers you might be using a 7-foot-6-inch to 9-foot leader. For wet flies in general, you'll be using a 3X tippet most of the time; for nymphs, probably a 4X tippet.

Feeding Fish

88 percent under the film

12 percent on the film

Wet flies are very effective since fish feed under the water most of the time.

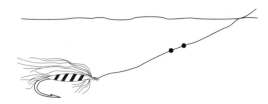

Apply shot as needed to achieve the desired depth for your wet fly. Some flies are already weighted (with wraps of lead). Some casters don't like weighted flies because they feel it affects drifts, so they use shot instead. Everyone has an opinion; you'll have to decide for yourself.

Spools of Leader. You'll likely carry spools of leader when you're fly casting. As you tie on flies, the tippet gets worn down. For wet-fly casting, you may want spools of leader that are heavier than for dry-fly fishing since you'll be using a heavier line. You'll also want a stiffer, heavier line for times that you fish two flies. For your second *dropper,* you'll want a stiffer line. A dropper is a second line added to the leader that will allow you to fish two flies. Keep the dropper short so it won't get twisted around on the leader. A stiff leader for the dropper also really helps.

Lead Weight. You'll also need some lead, probably split shot. There's a lot of discussion on weighted flies. Some casters, especially Michael, think a weighted fly adversely affects the action and the drift. If you are in this camp, you definitely need something to weigh down your leader. Even if you do fish weighted flies, there are times when the tiny wraps of lead are not enough to get your fly to the bottom, so you'll need to add extra weight anyway. Any fishing store that caters to fly fishing, and most that don't, will carry micro shot. Don't buy the stuff bait fishermen use because the shot is too big. Get an assorted box with lots of different sizes. The largest shot will be a little larger than a BB; the smallest will be very tiny and is often called micro shot. Get the most expensive stuff they have; you'll thank yourself for it later. Cheap shot is cut poorly and is difficult to open up. You'll waste half of it trying to get it open and on the line—and then it won't stay on long. (It's always amusing to see a guy in a tackle shop who owns a $400 rod and a $200 reel but is worried about saving a few quarters on split shot.)

Strike Indicators. There are dozens of different strike indicators on the market, bobbers, for example, that are items designed to stay on top of the water to give you a visible indication of when a fish has taken your fly. It is best to avoid strike indicators that look like a little piece of hollow fly line that fits

The Strike Indicator

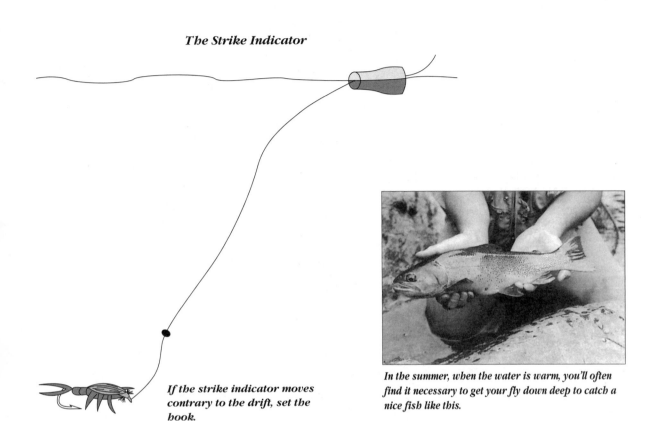

If the strike indicator moves contrary to the drift, set the book.

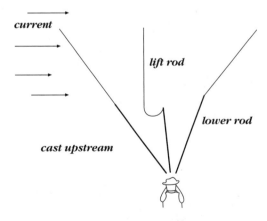

In the summer, when the water is warm, you'll often find it necessary to get your fly down deep to catch a nice fish like this.

Controlling the Rod

current

lift rod

lower rod

cast upstream

Cast upstream and take up the slack as the fly drifts. As the fly drifts toward you, lower the rod. As the fly drifts away from you, raise the rod.

like a sleeve up your leader. Yes, these are more delicate and they do make casting a little easier, but they are more difficult to use and will result in fewer catches for you. Instead, use one of the many sticky-sided, high-density models you can attach anywhere on the leader (like the Umpqua Roll On). These are disposable. Once you stick one on, it's pretty much stuck there. If you shift to a different depth of water, you can sometimes move it up or down, but usually you have to tear it off and stick on a new indicator. Another style—a rather oblong model with a hollow core and a rubber band in the middle—is a little bulkier, especially for casting. They come in different sizes; arm yourself with small, medium, and large. Their advantage is that they can be moved up and down without having to tear them apart. Our

Across and Down

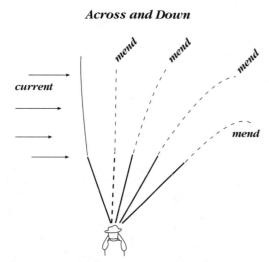

Cast across and let the current take the fly. As the line extends, the fly lifts and swings in.

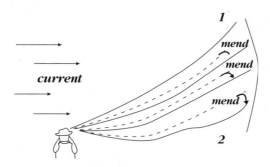

A different modification is needed when you cast across and downstream. Mend as needed as your fly drifts.

favorite strike indicator, without a doubt, is a piece of poly (rubbed with a fair bit of floatant). It can be easily seen, and it rides on the water very nicely. The slightest pickup will be seen.

Successful Casts to Consider

We'll show you several casts to use in wet-fly fishing. They are all successful, but some work better on some waters than others. The rule to remember is: *Fish the water consistently and thoroughly.*

Across and Down

This is the classic way to throw a wet fly.

If you understand a little bit about mending line, if you can lob out a bunch of line (even if it slaps the water), if you can lift your rod up, if you can strip back some line . . . you are ready to catch a lot of fish. It takes a few minutes to learn this cast well enough to be instantly successful. It takes a lifetime to master.

Sometimes this is called the "downward swing." This is an especially good technique when you are fishing attractor patterns. Cast outward or slightly downstream. Allow the current to sweep your fly. At first your pattern will sink as it's swept away. Let it get carried down. As it reaches the end, the belly of your line will tighten and the fly will start to rise and swing back. While the fly is floating, and especially during the swing, you might lift the rod, twitch, strip the line back toward you, or let it swing naturally. Pick up the line, cast over the water, and let your fly drift downstream.

A fish can hit anytime, so you have to be ready to set the hook if need be. Most often the strike will occur when the fly is in the swing motion. Perhaps the fish feels the fly is getting away during the lift or swing, and it triggers something that makes the fish strike. When you are done, take three steps downstream and fish the section you just fished.

You can extend the drift. If you decide you want to let your fly drift farther, feed some additional line to the slack and let the current take it. As you feed out the line, twitch (shake) the rod slowly. Fish will hit hard. A soft rod will make it easier on your tippet. Use a slip strike to set the hook (let the line partly slip through your finger on the rod). The fish will set itself.

The Upstream Wedge

The old standby cast, the cast that may have accounted for the most fish with a wet fly, is the upstream cast. You cast upstream and take up the slack line. This cast is often referred to as the ten-o'clock-to-two-o'clock cast. What you'll be doing is fishing upstream in a wedge based on the hour locations on a clock. You'll stand facing directly upstream. You'll start casting at ten o'clock, letting the fly drift back to you with the current while you strip in the slack. Next you'll move to ten-thirty, letting the line drift back to you while you take up the slack. You'll work your way across to two o'clock.

From here you can fish the wedge again and again if you're over a good spot, move to your left or right and fish water you've missed, or move upstream 5 feet and start the process over again.

There are a number of different casting strategies for wet casting, but if you never went beyond the upstream wedge, you'd catch lots of fish. The secret, as with dry fishing, is to get the right drift.

Your fly must drift naturally. Remember that you'll have to contend with a lot of different currents. Drag isn't as critical a factor as it is with dry-fly casting, but it is important. You don't want the fly line to belly and pull your fly out of the drift or the strike zone.

Watch the currents. You'll need to mend to keep your fly in the right path. One of the best ways to keep your fly in check is to keep an eye on your strike indicator. You can't see the bottom of the

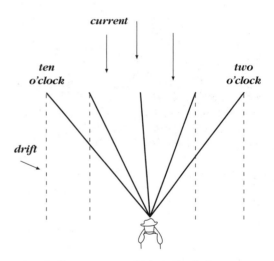

The Upstream Wedge Cast (ten o'clock to two o'clock)

Cast the line upstream and take in the slack.

This nice brown was caught on weighted black leach using an upstream wedge with a twitch. Michael picked up this beauty in the Provo River on the first cast.

stream, so all you can do is watch the surface. The best way to keep your system in order is to keep the strike indicator floating exactly with the current. Look at bubbles and drifting leaves or wood. Your indicator should be floating even with the current— not slower or faster. (If you can't get the drift right, slower is better than faster because the current will be slower on the bottom than on top.) If your indicator is moving differently from the current, you probably won't get much fishing action. (Throw in a serpentine cast to help do away with the drag.)

If you find the drift is still off after proper mending, adjust the weight. If you have too much weight on, it will slow your fly down too much. Adjusting the weight is a continuing process as you fish different water and currents.

The Upstream Wedge with a Twitch

Sometimes you'll fish a wet fly that you don't want to float with the drift (especially streamers or bucktails). You'll still want to cast upstream, but instead of letting the current carry the fly, you'll supply the action.

To do this you'll need to strip a little bit faster. Keep the fly moving just a little bit faster than the current. You might move your rod tip from side to side to give the fly added action.

The twitch works well in water that isn't moving too fast.

The Lift Cast

This cast is excellent when you want your fly to float downstream in a roughly straight line. The lift from the bottom at the end of the drift is a great triggering device. Cast upstream to the two o'clock position and let the fly sink. By the time the fly gets to the bottom at three o'clock or three-thirty, mend the line to keep the drift natural. When the fly is at four o'clock, lift the rod. The fly will look like it's rising to the surface to emerge.

Beaver Pond Dead Drift

This is a superb cast (strategy) for fishing slow, clear water, especially when you can see fish moving about that aren't breaking the surface. It's very effective in beaver ponds, lakes, or slow streams.

Start with a 9- to 12-foot leader and a dry fly. Yes, a dry fly that floats well, like a Royal Wulff, a Humpy, or a Coachman. Tie the dry fly to the end of the tippet. Treat the dry fly with floatant. It needs to float well. Now tie on 2 to 3 feet of lighter tippet (6X or 7X) directly to the bend of the hook.

Tie on a small nymph such as a Pheasant Tail #18 to #20, a Serendipity #18 to #22, or a Scud #12 to #20. (Match as close to the natural as you can.) Add a micro shot about 6 inches above the nymph.

Dead drift to a point near or above visible fish or where you think the fish are. Watch the dry fly. It will be your strike indicator—and it will take an occasional fish, also.

The Beaver Pond Dead Drift

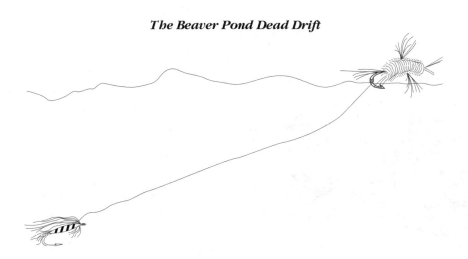

Setting the Hook

Setting the hook will make or break you on catching fish. Even though you'll often be using a strike indicator when wet-fly casting, you can't see what is going on under the water. With a dry fly, you'll often see the fish take your fly—but not so with a wet fly.

When in doubt, set the hook!

If you suspect that a fish has taken the fly, set the hook. If you feel any sort of bump (even if it might just be from your fly or shot on a rock), set the hook. If your strike indicator moves to the left or the right, upstream or downstream, set the hook. If the strike indicator moves oddly in any way, set the hook. Yes, you're going to pick up frequent snags on rocks or the moss—but you'll also be hooking more fish.

You don't need to slam the hook. Just lift the rod quickly and take up the slack. If you slam it, you might snap the leader.

When in doubt, set the hook. It is our opinion that fish examine, mouth, and spit your fly dozens of times a day. And the angler never knows.

The Wet-Fly Approach

We have defined the term *wet-fly fishing* to mean fishing under the surface of the water. It also has a more limited meaning as a catch-all name for fishing with general attractor (impressionistic) wet flies. (This excludes the nymphs and streamers we'll discuss next.) It's a general sort of approach to casting that is more or less directed and planned, depending on the skills of the caster.

This approach often involves a caster tying on two or three different flies at the same time, choosing among such files as a Coachman, a Gnat, a Yellow Hackle, a smaller Wooly Bugger, a Renegade, an Ant, a Royal Wulff, and dozens of others. You jump in the water and see how it works.

Dave trained his son early how to work a wet fly. You can't buy a smile like this.

The better you read water, the better you fish. You might employ any of the casting strategies we've suggested. You're fishing with general attractors, but over the course of the day you can be pretty successful. Most casters work their flies up and across and down. If you don't have success with the regular across-and-down in this style of fishing, twitch and lift the rod on the swing.

This kind of wet-fly casting has come to mean tying on a few likely flies, plunging into the water, and casting wherever the hell you please without a thought. It's referred to by many in the Rocky Mountain West as "toss that pattern an' pray!" This has caused some of the purist dry-fly folk to look down their very insolent noses. But while this certainly isn't fishing with a plan, fish still get caught this way, and people have enough success to keep doing it.

Most of the "toss that pattern an' pray" folks would like to fish with a plan and with a few casting strategies. They just don't know where to start—and this sport isn't always as beginner-friendly as it ought to be.

Patterns you should collect for general wet-fly fishing include the Soft Hackle Hare's Ear #12 to #18, the Gray or Brown Hackle Peacock #12 to #18, and the Gray Hackle Yellow #12 to #18.

Nymphing Approach

What a way to catch fish. Lots of fish.

When a fly caster mentions nymphing, he or she is talking about nymph-stage bugs: immature insects. Nymphs that are swept into streams make tempting treats for trout.

In his book *The Trout and the Stream,* Charles Brooks advises: "Fish where the food is." This is an essential concept. If you can't find the fish, as you would when dry-fly casting, go where you know there's food: the bottom. And repeatedly, this means nymphs.

Kick around on the rocks, dislodge some

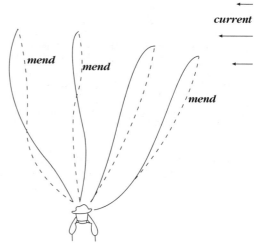

Mending Wets for Success

To successfully fish a nymph or other wet fly on a dead drift, you have to continually mend the line to meet the demands of the current.

This large fish was taken on a small fly. The trout in this section of river were "locked up"... or so it was said. The problem: Most casters were using flies that were too large. A #22 Griffiths Gnat took this fish and many others like it. When other casters went to smaller patterns, they caught fish, too.

When you are wading, look for places that provide food, comfort, and safety for the fish. Then present what they are taking in a natural way.

structure, and use your insect net to find out what's going on in the stream. If you can find out what sort of nymph activity is going on and then use flies that match the nymphs in size, shape, and color, your fishing average will increase because you'll be fishing with a plan.

Some experts say wet-fly fishing with nymphs is the most demanding form of fly fishing. All we can say is that we must be fishing on different rivers. To fish nymphs well takes a lot of skill, but so does dry-fly casting, wet-fly casting with streamers, etc. Such experts suggest you have to *precisely* match the nymph to be successful. But you don't. The key word is *impression,* not exact copy. The closer you get to the natural offerings, of course, the better, but it's not critical that you match up exactly. Look at size, shape, and color—but usually an impressionistic wet-fly pattern will be enough. How you fish the fly is more important than a precise match with the natural. In other words, presentation is everything.

The first and last rule about nymphing is to have the nymphs drift naturally in the current.

If you were a foolish nymph who pushed the limits of your world and crawled onto a rock and were swept away in the current, where would you tumble? The answer is: close to the bottom. Therefore, when you drift your nymph, keep it as close to the bottom as you can. It's a more natural drift this way.

As your nymph pattern is swept downstream, it should be so close to the bottom that it occasionally bumps the rocks. This is called "bouncing the nymph."

A natural drift can't be emphasized enough. On one productive section of a small river, Dave was guiding two clients. Both were about equal in skill, competent dry-fly casters but fairly new to the wet-fly game. To show how important drift is, Dave took both men to a fine stretch of water, where he cast upstream near a large rock and let the fly drift through the water. Nothing happened. The fly was just under the surface. Then he added a piece of lead shot and cast again. Still nothing. The fly was deeper but not deep enough. Dave added one more shot and said, "This should be about right. This should take the fly down deep enough." Halfway into the strike zone, his rod bowed and he reeled in a fat 15-inch brown.

"Was it luck?" he asked. "Most of the skill is getting the fly to bump across the bottom." He moved up and repeated the exercise. On the third cast, after adding enough weight, he caught another fish. The lesson was vivid. *You have to get the fly down.* This often means experimenting with the shot until you get the right combination.

Keep that nymph bumping across the bottom of the stream.

The exception to the bottom rule is when nymphs start to emerge. At this time, use less weight so the pattern can rise up and down naturally in the current. At the same time, you can manipulate the natural drift and lift your rod tip gradually. This simulates the emerger coming to the surface. An emergence can trigger a trout attack.

Now that we have covered some of the general concepts of nymph fishing, let's look at some effective ways to cast the nymph.

Up and Across. This is a good way to present your nymph. Cast your fly upstream and across from wherever you are standing. Let the line drift downstream past you. Mend the line as needed, keeping an eye on the indicator so that you are getting an accurate drift. Turn to face the fly as it drifts downstream. When the fly is in front of you, lift your rod to take in slack; then lower it as the fly continues downstream. As the line fully extends, and the fly starts its swing, cast upstream again and start over.

The Upstream Wedge. The wedge (the ten-o'clock-to-two-o'clock cast) is a good place to start, especially if you are on a stream with a uniform flow. Some consider this a difficult way to fish because it is hard to detect a strike, but it's likely the

This fish was caught on a Hare's Ear that drifted over a likely lie.

Fishing Nymph Emergers

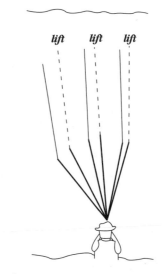

To simulate an emerging nymph, lift the rod.

Study the current so you'll know how to work your streamer. It's likely you'll have to experiment with it until you get the action that will attract fish.

easiest way to get a smooth drift. It's necessary to keep the slack out of the line and to set the hook at the first indication of a strike. Otherwise the fish will spit the hook before you know it's there.

The Lift Cast. An emerging nymph is an excellent trigger for trout. The lift cast simulates the rising of a nymph to the surface to emerge. Review the lift cast described earlier in this chapter.

Some Nymphs to Consider

There are a thousand nymph patterns you can tie or purchase. We'd like to suggest a few so you can start off with a bang. Armed with these patterns, you can handle most fishing situations.

Caddis Nymphs. As you know, matching the size is the most critical element. The major colors you'll be concerned with are green, brown, and light caramel, although the colors and tones may vary with different locations. The Gold Ribbed Hare's Ear and the Muskrat Nymph are good flies in sizes #14 to #18.

Stone fly Nymphs. Select colors from dark brown to black.

Mayfly Nymphs. Select colors from dark brown to light brown to gray.

Streamers

The word *streamer* refers to a category of wet fly: the bigger, heavier fly. There's a lot of body, so it "streams"; it's streamlined in the water. The major element of a streamer is the wing (the bulk that undulates in the water).

There are two types of streamers. To confuse matters, one type also has the name "streamer." This type consists of a flowing wing—usually of marabou, feather, or synthetic—that's quite bulky when dry but that becomes small when wet. It moves in the water and has a lifelike appearance. Some refer to this movement as a "breathing"

*Wet Fly: Steady Swim Retrieves
for Large/Smallmouth Bass*

*Strip in 1 to 3 inches at a time in steady movements, and
the pattern will come in evenly.*

*Wet Fly: Intermediate Regular Dive Retrieve
for Large/Smallmouth Bass*

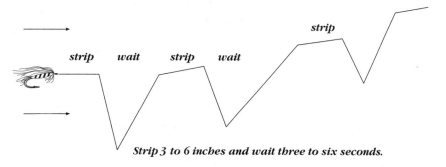

Strip 3 to 6 inches and wait three to six seconds.

*Wet Fly: Deep Water Retrieve
for Long Casts*

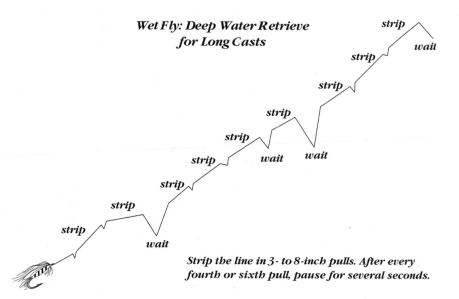

*Strip the line in 3- to 8-inch pulls. After every
fourth or sixth pull, pause for several seconds.*

motion. When the fly is pulled through the water, the feathers pull inward. When the fly is stopped, the feathers float out.

Another type of streamer is the bucktail. This fly is often made of deer hair, but any animal hair can be employed. At first glance, a bucktail looks sparse. But it doesn't clump down. It is the same size in the water as it is when dry. This fly has a pulsing motion when pulled through the water and fast bursts when stopped.

Most people use the word *streamer* in referring to the fly that becomes smaller when wet or to the bucktail fly. This is the broader, more general definition that we'll use throughout this section.

Among fly fishers, nymph fishing has become "respectable," while streamer casting has been looked down upon by the sport's "proper" casters. Somehow, imitating a nymph or a caddis or a mayfly was thought to be of a higher order than imitating a fish with a streamer. Few people thought much about streamers. Sure, everyone had a few in their fly boxes, but they usually rusted from disuse. Only a few people used them (those fallen from the dry-casting faith). They apparently used them well, as evidenced by the numbers of fish they caught. The streamer casters began catching large fish, and the trend didn't go unnoticed. We're talking about *big* fish; good-size trophy fish. Now, throwing a streamer is almost thought of as normal.

Streamers are flies that you, as the caster, give life to. You'll catch fewer fish than with smaller flies—but the fish you catch will be big. As a fish grows, it starts moving up the food chain. In addition to insects and aquatic life, a larger fish looks for food that will give it more return for the energy it expends. This means other fish, such as char, shiner, sculpin, or baby trout, or perhaps leeches, tadpoles, frogs, and snakes—any sort of solid food.

This is where streamers come in. A streamer imitates something large, an item of food that a larger fish might be interested in. Streamers look like fish in the water, soft and alive.

Fishing the Streamer

Most of these patterns are tied on extended shank hooks. These aren't delicate patterns. They are bulky and heavy. You have to throw them with a wide loop (no tight loops like those you'd use for a midge).

How do you fish a streamer? Remember, you give it its life (though once in a while you'll let the current help). Start by fishing the types of casts we have already described in this chapter. But instead of letting the streamer drift, strip in line and move the rod tip to give it action. Unless the fish are very aggressive, you'll want to slow down your pattern. Most beginning casters fish their streamers too fast. This is when you need to be very aware of the water temperature. If it is much higher or lower than the fish's optimum temperature, you're liable to have sluggish fish. A fish in this mode isn't going to expend much energy to get its dinner. If the water temperature is optimum, then a little more "action" to your pattern might prove to be effective.

Optimum presentation with a streamer means giving the fish a side view of the pattern.

Move the fly, let it drift, stop it. Make it look alive. It's not a problem if the pattern occasionally hits the bottom. Don't pull in the fly on a straight line. Make your streamer look like a wounded or injured fish; nothing triggers a large fish more quickly. With the tip of your rod, flip the pattern from side to side. At times, change direction entirely. Perhaps even let the tail drift with the current. Most good streamer casters experiment with their presentation. Be dynamic. Bass fishers who have used jigs take to streamer fishing very rapidly. They understand that the "life" in your pattern is you.

While you can do almost anything with a streamer, there are several "classic" casts or patterns we'd like to show you. The best presentation is usually a broadside view, providing more of the fly to see. To give the fish a broadside view, a swing pattern works best. One swing pattern is called the

Our friend Alan caught this fish on a rather large streamer. He worked it in a hurried manner, attracting this brown. It took Alan nearly twenty minutes to bring this fish to net because he was using very light leader.

Swinging a streamer can be deadly. Dave's son proudly holds up his catch.

swinging streamer; another is called the swinging dead drift.

Swinging Streamer

This is a cast to use when you don't want to go deep. It's an excellent way to cover the water by swinging the streamer across the current and tempting lunker trout. Angling downstream, cast the streamer and let it sink. Then direct the fly through the swing by working your rod tip or stripping the line. Give more action to the pattern by lifting and dropping your rod. (Mend now and then as needed.)

To get more depth, don't cast as far down the current. Cast across or perhaps slightly upstream. Let the pattern sink as the current takes it. As the line tightens, the fly will rise up and level off. This will attract fish in deeper water. This action of rising is a triggering device for trout and shouldn't be overlooked.

To cover a section of water thoroughly with the swing, do it both ways. If needed, add more weight to your line.

Swinging Dead Drift

Don't be fooled by the word *dead*. This isn't a "toss that pattern an' pray" cast. You need to constantly be alert. If you are going to cast a streamer on a dead drift, you'll have to concentrate. A strike is quick and fast. There's no time for a second chance.

What you are trying to do with the swinging dead drift is to keep the streamer moving so that fish have a broadside view of the fly. At the same time, the fly has to move naturally in the current.

Start by casting upstream. Next, you'll need to throw a mend on your line (mend the line upstream). Depending on the current you are fishing, you'll need to mend according to how fast your line bellies. This doesn't have to be a savage mend nor as delicate a mend as you'd throw with a dry fly. With your rod tip, flip your line upstream. *Keep mending to keep the fly drifting correctly.*

Swinging Dead Drift

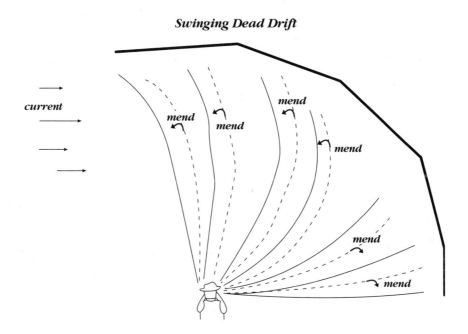

As the line reaches the end of its drift and tightens, the streamer will start to swing back toward you. If you allow the line to get too tight, the head of the streamer will be toward you, and the tail section will point downstream. To prevent this—so the streamer will go across the current broadside—*mend downstream.*

You are most likely to get a strike when the streamer is lifting into the swing or when it is broadside in the stream. This is a high-percentage time to pick up a fish. Be extra alert.

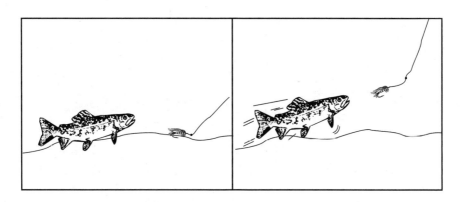

12

GOING HIGH AND DRY

Fishing the Dry Fly

Throwing dry flies may not be the oldest form of fly casting, but, by gosh, it's the way to show you've finally arrived.

Right or wrong, dry-fly fishing gets all the glory, all the status, and all the honor—never mind that wet flies will net you more fish. Even the true-blue nympher will admit that there's nothing in this world quite like casting a #20 fly 75 feet (a perfectly tight loop goes without saying) to a rising lunker brown taking caddis off the film. There's still a hint of morning mist in the air, and you can taste the heavy dew on your lips. The surface of the gin-clear water is polished like an expensive mirror. The hushed morning light dances into a million avenues once it hits the small lake. It's bright and focused out, not washed and dull like it will be at noon. The air is alpine sharp and almost bites as you take in deep breaths. Throwing dry flies makes you at one with the setting.

There's something about this setting that allows you to see more clearly how all the parts come together. The muscular brown rises to the Elk Hair you've tied. Seeing the splash, you lift the rod, take up the slack, and set the hook. The spotted trout with the square tail runs. You palm your reel to slow him down. You finally net the fighter, making

A proper drift with a dry fly is very important if you want to interest a wary fish.

It took Lee nearly a half hour to finally hook his fish with a dry. He changed flies six times until he matched the hatch with an exact presentation, a #20 Blue Wing Olive.

him yours. You release the hook, returning him to the water, and the cycle is complete.

Maybe it's hype and illusion. Maybe it's reality.

For us, however, it's more than reality. It simply is. It's magic. It's Santa Claus and wedding nights and mystery rolled into one. We don't recommend you give up wet-fly fishing, because it's glorious, too, but in other ways than dry-fly fishing (the main one being catching more fish). But when the fish are hitting on the surface, drop everything you're doing and pick up your rod.

Historians of fly fishing have traced dry-fly casting back hundreds of years (wet-fly fishing goes back thousands). The sport as we know it today probably had its roots in the south of England on clear-flowing, nutrient-enriched, spring-fed, temperate chalk streams. The fish in these meandering streams were easy to find, but they were incredibly spooky. Because the water was very clear and rich in food, English brown trout were selective. The British casters had to be exact, or they went away empty-handed. The techniques British casters used were readily applied on American waters a little more than a hundred years ago but had to be modified somewhat.

Such modification, no doubt, caused the chalk-water-stream aristocrat to look down his nose at the casters in the colonies. And with good reason. Our water is a lot swifter, and a number of changes had to be made, or we wouldn't be catching fish.

Needless to say, dry-fly casting is the highest form, *the only form,* of casting—or so the snobs have tried to convince us. We still don't do it right, according to the British, but perhaps they're still a little bitter over the colony issue. While you'll probably enjoy more initial fishing success with a wet fly, there's something about dry-fly fishing that really hooks you. Once you get it under your skin, it never goes away. You won't be throwing dry flies perfectly overnight, but you'll feel very cozy, in a traditional sort of way, every time you cast.

Unlike wet-fly fishing, dry casting makes the act of casting itself a critical element. Getting the fly in the right direction isn't enough. You must cast with precision.

Just like wet fishing, dry fishing is determined mostly by *manner*, not always by the actual pattern, or fly, itself. In other words, *how* you're fishing the fly is the determining factor. If you're fishing on the film, you're fishing dry. If you're fishing under the film, you're fishing wet.

Still, there are some basic differences between wet-fly and dry-fly patterns, even if there is a fair amount of crossover. Nevertheless, in a generic sort of way, dry-fly hackles are often hard (taken from cocks instead of hens). Dry flies also employ more hackle to help the fly float on the film and give it good visibility. The wings are often tied high, and the hook is generally light.

Dry-fly fishing means intense casting. You can't make mistakes without scaring fish.

Fishing wet, at least from a casting perspective, isn't nearly as difficult as fishing dry. Throwing dry flies is a more skilled endeavor. A wet-fly cast can be less than precise, and you still won't scare the fish. If you cast poorly or slap the water, you're not likely to scare the fish because they're in deep water and aren't as apprehensive as they would be on or near the surface. And while you have to pay attention to the drag with different styles of wet casting, it isn't as critical as in throwing dry flies.

When you cast dries, you have to be more exacting. Because the fish are near the surface, you have to cast so the line doesn't hit the water or drop down too close to a feeding fish. A great deal of your fishing effort is spent getting the line in the right place, and the margin for error is narrow. One mistake, and the fish are gone. When you fish dries, you'll want to match the food the fish are eating as closely as you can, unless you are fishing an impressionistic pattern.

Dave admires a nice fish before sending it home.

Fish feed on the film only 10 to 20 percent of the time. This is why a dry-fly caster has to fish with a plan to be successful when the fish are rising.

In this chapter, we'll discuss how to set up to fish flies dry and offer some basic dry-fly casting and fishing strategies.

How to Get Set Up

Your regular fly rod will do just fine if you've followed our suggestions in chapter 2 for selecting a rod. And you'll need a floating line, which you also learned about in that chapter.

Most of the time you'll be using a 9-foot leader tapered down 3X to 6X. (You'll probably want to use a 4X and go with a fine tippet during the low water of summer on spring creeks and with midges.) A fine tippet gives you a fine presentation and likely more strikes, but you're going to lose more fish to break-offs. It's also more forgiving on drag. A limp leader lands a little more loosely, with more curve. As a result, the current will move it before the fly.

As you tie on flies, the tippet gets worn down, so you'll likely carry extra spools of tippet. This will save you money because you won't have to tie on a new tapered leader every time you use up the bottom section. And there are times you'll want to lengthen your leader by tying on additional tippet or additional lighter tippet.

Basic Dry-Fly Fishing Strategies

You have reviewed chapter 3 and have practiced the basic casts, so you have a working knowledge of how to move your fly line around. Later in this chapter, we are going to show you several styles of dry-fly casting, approaches to help you cast successfully in almost any water. First, let's talk about some basic dry-fly strategies.

Placing the Fly

With a wet fly, you don't care how the fly or line hits the water. The fish are down deep, and the little bit of commotion your line makes likely won't make any difference. But with dries, you want your fly to float down to the water. If you slap the water or even come down too hard, you've got problems. Remember, the fish are near the surface. And since they are near the surface and not in a safety zone, they're much more prone to being spooked. The slightest mistake will send them to the moss, under a rock, or down deep.

It won't matter if your fly is on target; if you spook the fish, it's gone. Practice casting your line so it floats down and hits the water like a snowflake. When you are fishing close, you'll very likely be able to achieve a soft line drop. When you cast farther out, you're liable to *smack* the film. This often occurs when a caster is pushing his or her limits.

Don't fish beyond your casting skills. Sneak up close so that you'll have a greater chance of fooling the fish. If the fish are spooky at all, a badly placed line will mean goodbye to your chance of a hookup.

It's fun to cast a long way. But any casting expert will tell you that if you have a chance of getting close to a fish, do it. The closer you are, the more likely you'll land the fish. Even if you can drop a fly above a likely lie from 96 feet, it's hard to hook the fish. With a lot of line on the water, it's tough setting the hook. There's slack line to contend with, and the leader is still so delicate that you can easily snap it. If a long cast is the only way you can fish a certain water, do it. Otherwise, get closer.

Accuracy in casting is essential. You are casting to feeding fish in a stream, or where you think feeding fish will be. You have to practice getting into the strike zone. Generally, if you can get your fly within a 25-inch circle around the fish, you're in the strike zone. If you can get your fly within a 15-inch circle around the fish, so much the better. Sometimes even

Fish-Eye View: "The Window"

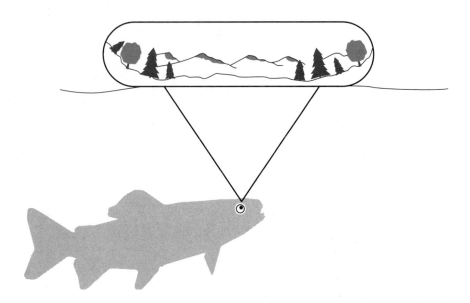

this isn't enough. Occasionally you'll have to get your fly nearly over the fish for a take.

Overcasting is a major problem. Get the fly, not the line, over the strike zone.

You need to judge distance and know what it takes to get your fly to your target. A little practice will make you good in a hurry, especially if you think about what you are doing. Even then it can be tricky. Take a practice cast if you can. Find a target to the right or to the left, far enough away so you won't disturb the feeding fish. Cast to it and make the mental adjustments. If this doesn't work, cast short. You won't hurt anything, and it will tell you how much more line it will take to get into the strike zone. If you can cast upstream and not worry about your line, do so (mending as the fly floats into the strike zone).

You'll notice how much better you're casting after you practice. You'll also notice how many more fish you're catching. The one fly in the ointment is wind, which can foul your cast and presentation in a hurry. To the zephyrs, try a side cast to get lower to the water. On the Green River, not far from our homes, afternoon wind is to be planned on. If you don't have a side cast, you won't be casting very far.

Opening the Window

When a fish looks up at the surface, it sees a distorted-on-edges cone. This is referred to as a *window*. This cone of view is the trout's picture of the surface film and the outside world. (For camera buffs, this is where we get the term *fish-eye lens*.)

This window is important because it helps a trout keep an eye out for predators. It also allows the fish to spot food floating on the film or flying just above it.

The closer the fish is to the surface, the smaller its window is. Fish feeding on the surface usually hold in the lie fairly close to the film. Ideally, you'll want to land your fly just upstream of the window or the line of sight so the fly can quickly drift into the fish's sight. (We sometimes refer to the window as the *strike zone* or *sight zone*.) The longer the fly has to float, the longer you have to worry about drag. A good rule of thumb is to land your fly about 2 to 3 feet upstream from the window.

This means you'll have to work on accuracy. Practice on the lawn with a pie plate at 20 to 50 feet. Start close. When you can hit the plate with a minimum of false casts, move 5 feet back. When you can cast 40 to 50 feet accurately, you'll be ready for even the toughest spring creek.

Watching the Drag

Repeat after us: When casting a dry fly, it's a sin to let the fly drag. Always work for a natural drift. *It's a sin to drag.*

It takes some practice setting the hook. No matter how long you've been fishing, a few are going to get away. This one didn't.

A boat is a handy fishing tool. It's a good way to cover a lot of water.

Setting the Hook

As we pointed out in the chapter on wet-fly fishing, setting the hook will make or break you when it comes to catching fish.

With a dry fly you'll often see the fish take your fly. There's always a little lag time involved. You've got just an instant to set the hook, so you have to practice being quick. When you see the fish move toward what looks like your fly, or you see a fish on the surface near your fly, or you see a splash by your fly, *lift the rod* and set the hook. A firm lift is all you need—it doesn't have to be a hard jerk. A bit of steel and feather doesn't taste natural to a trout. As soon as it clamps down, it'll spit your hook out and take off. Your job is to drive the point through its lip before it gets a chance to swim off.

Sometimes you aren't sure. It'll look like the fish is just a few inches or a foot away from your fly. Set the hook anyway. They aren't streamlined for nothing. They can dart through water rapidly. You may think you know where your fly is, but the fish may already have picked up or spit the hook and started to swim away before you see it or it makes a splash. Set the hook. Sure, you're going to be wrong every now and then and maybe grab some air, but you're going to be right more often than not and have something to show for it.

Again, when setting the hook, *a simple lift of the rod will do.* You're trying to take the slack out of the line. Don't yank back like a bass fisherman with a spinning outfit! A light tippet requires only a light touch. And a light lift, in case you grab air, won't be as likely to spook the fish.

When in doubt, lift the rod!

But remember that there's not much give in a fly line. There's some give in a leader toward the tippet, but not much before it snaps. You must exercise care, or you are going to break the tippet. There isn't leeway for a hearty yank.

The points on your hooks should be sharpened each time you use them. To test them, see if they'll prick the edge of your fingernail and hang with little pressure. A sharp hook means a lot more fish since it will do half the work for you.

The trick is taking up the slack so the hook can do its job. You want to take the slack out of the line so the trout is hooked and can't spit the hook while you are playing it in. It goes without saying that the lighter the tippet, the more gently you're going to have to lift. It takes a little bit of practice. You'll snap the leader a time or two before you get the fine touch honed down.

Even then, you're still going to break line. Here's a little story to show my point: We were invited to fish at some private ponds one winter day. They hadn't been fished much, but the fish turned out to be more wary than you'd think. The browns and 'bows were cagey, and we had to lighten up our leaders considerably. To catch fish, we used a 5X to a 6X leader. This is a pretty thin leader for fish in murky pond conditions. We got a lot of tag-ups, but lost many fish by breaking the tippet when setting the hook. The point is, we all break off our fair share, especially when the fish are large but conditions require that you go very light. The average fish we hooked was more than two pounds; a few were more than five pounds. We went through yards of leader.

The Good Time to Fish

When is a good time to fish?

Anytime you can fish, you should.

You owe it to yourself—and you owe it to those around you. A fished person is a happy person, a more productive worker, a better citizen, a better spouse, a better parent, a better human being.

Any fishing is better than no fishing. And since you'll soon start to feel that fishing is intricately connected to your self-worth, it won't matter when, as long as you do.

But what about when you have a choice? What time should you choose for fishing?

Spring fishing in Utah. It sometimes means a little bit of snow—but the fishing is good. You should fish anytime you can!

You don't have to get up at the crack of dawn to catch fish. More often than not, the best fishing occurs when you are the most comfortable. This fish was caught on the Green River in Utah during the middle of the day.

There's something to be said for getting up at the crack of dawn and hitting the water. All the old fishing tales seem to suggest that you have to be there at first light to get your fish. And sometimes this is true. Dave is naturally an early riser. But if you're like Michael and hate getting up in the morning, you won't be disappointed. You don't have to beat the rooster up to catch good fish most of the time as a fly caster. When is the best time to be on the water so you can enjoy good fishing? Adjust your fishing to the times the flies or hatches are on the water.

To be victorious as a dry-fly caster, you first have to have a couple of things working together. The water conditions have to be conducive: temperatures, water levels, oxygen. (A spring run-off or high water due to a week of summer rain won't help you.) And the conditions have to be such as to cause mature insects to hatch and spawn in workable amounts that excite fish.

Then you can decide on the time of day. For that purpose, Dave has an approach that Michael lives by (since it justifies his sleeping in). Here is the "Dave Card Rule for Bugs":

> The best fishing is usually when you are the most comfortable. In the fall and spring, it's best around noon when it's not too cool. In the summer, it's best in the mornings and evenings when it's not too hot. Whatever time of the day you feel the most comfortable, not being too hot or too cold, will be the best time of day for the bugs . . . and thus, the fish.

Isn't that nice. You don't have to beat the sun up to catch fish.

Useful Dry-Fly Casts

Now let's get down to the real dry-fly fishing business at hand and put the pieces together. Let's discuss dry-fly casts we think you'll find successful.

Some casts are modifications on the wet-fly casts we talked about in the last chapter. These casting ideas will help you become successful as a dry-fly caster, although some work better on some waters than others. The rule to remember is to fish the water consistently and thoroughly.

When fishing, you'll either cast to water where you think fish might be or cast to water where you see fish rising. It would be nice to always fish for trout we see feeding near the surface, but that's not always in the cards. We'll cover strategies for the various scenarios you might encounter.

Alan took this fish with a quartering cast.

As you're aware, having a soft delivery and an accurate cast is very important to a dry-fly fisher. It's nice to throw hundred-foot casts, and it's something you can do with practice. But most of the time you'll be fishing at less than 50 feet away. Most of the trout that casters catch are between 25 and 35 feet away. For every time you cast out 80 feet, there will be countless times a good, accurate 30-foot cast will bring home the bacon.

You may get tired of hearing us talk about drag-free casts and drifts. But it's too important not to repeat.

Drag is the black plague of fly casting; it wipes out a third to a half of all casters from the beginning. The first step is your initial cast. Cast to reduce as much drag on the fly as you can. Second, mend to keep the drift of the fly natural.

Fast water poses an interesting drag situation. An advantage is that the water of the fish's window is breaking, so the fish have a hard time seeing you. You can practically get right over them before they spook. In this situation, you'll often use only a few feet of line; the rest will be leader. You can overcome the drag problem by avoiding it entirely. Simply lift the rod so most or all the line is off the water. Guide the leader about with the tip of your rod.

At other times you'll need to have a little line out. If you're not careful, fast water can pull at your line or leader and cause it to cut across the current. Sometimes in fast water you barely have time to mend. Luckily, the strike zone is generally a small area; the fly is over it and gone. In situations like this, throw a slack cast (a serpentine cast). The problem is that quick water takes the mend out fast. Throw enough slack so the fly floats naturally over your target area. Wait an instant, then pick it up.

Quartering Cast

Casting straight upstream isn't practical for a number of reasons. Sometimes it's hard to keep a natural drift if the current below the target zone is fast. Perhaps you want your fly—but not the line or leader—to float over the strike zone. Cast over the strike zone with a quarter cast, casting from two o'clock to four o'clock.

A fast current below the strike zone can pose a horrible problem for mending. No matter how carefully you throw a slack cast, no matter how well you're able to mend, it's still hard to keep a natural drift when you cast straight upstream. Sometimes when you cast up and over the fish, you spook them. It's obvious you don't want the fly line itself to be over the fish, but sometimes the fish will see the fly, come up to take it, and slam right into your tippet. Now, tippet is pretty light stuff, but to a fish, this is a signal that something is wrong.

A quartering cast often helps the mending problem. More important, you can drift your fly through the strike zone without line or leader problems because you are coming to the fish from an angle.

Reach Cast

To get an even better float, review the section in chapter 3 on the reach cast. Try casting directly upstream with a reach cast. This helps in water with tricky currents that cause mending problems.

The Upstream Wedge

The upstream wedge cast that we described in the chapter on wet-fly fishing also works great with dry fishing. This is where you cast upstream and take up the slack line. It's the cast also referred to as the ten-o'clock-to-two-o'clock cast. You'll start casting to ten o'clock, letting the fly drift back to you with the current while you strip in the slack. Next you'll cast to ten-thirty, and again let the line drift back to you while you take up the slack. You'll cast your way across to two o'clock.

You can then fish the wedge again and again. If you're over a good spot, move to your left or right and fish water you've missed. Or you can move up 5 feet and start the process over again.

There are numerous strategies for dry casting, but if you never go beyond the upstream wedge, you'll still catch lots of fish. The secret, as we've suggested over and over again, is getting the right drift. Your fly must drift naturally.

Watch the currents. Mend to keep your fly in the right path. Keep an eye on how your fly is floating. With proper mending, you'll get the drift right most of the time.

Abbey caught this fish on her favorite dry fly, the Royal Coachman.

The Upstream Wedge with a Twitch

Sometimes you'll fish a dry fly that you don't want to float with the drift: a caddis, a terrestrial, or an attractor. You'll still want to cast upstream, but instead of letting the current carry the fly, you'll supply the action. (This cast also was described in the chapter on wet-fly fishing.)

To do this, you'll need to strip faster. Keep the fly moving just a little bit faster than the current. Perhaps you'll want to move your rod tip from side to side to give the fly added action. The twitch works well in water that isn't moving too fast.

Downstream Cast

Cast straight downstream. Check your cast by pulling back as the fly is settling. Slowly lower the rod as the drift indicates. Shake out additional line to continue the drift. This way the fly gets to the fish before the leader.

Casting to Fish You See Rising

When you see trout working the surface, you know where to focus. It's a sign telling you that this is where the fish are; stop here and fish. It means that fish are aggressive, that there's some sort of hatch or hatches on, and the dinner bell is ringing. Rising trout are either selective or nonselective in their choice of food. If the fish are selective, match the hatch as closely as you can. If they aren't selective, give them something that looks like food and enjoy the moment.

Nonselective Fish

For these fish, any of the attractor patterns we've talked about will do nicely. These are hungry fish that are going for food. There may be more than one hatch on. The point is, they probably aren't triggered by any one specific insect.

The important thing is they are feeding actively. Our choice would be to start with the following five attractor patterns: the Adams, the Royal Coachman, the Royal Wulff, the Humpy, and the Irresistible. The main thing to keep in mind is that you must present naturally so the fish think your pattern is a natural insect. Avoid any drag in your float.

If all else fails, go with a terrestrial pattern, a pattern that is a little bit different. Or perhaps try the Wulff or Coachman a bit larger, maybe in a #12.

Selective Fish

As you know, you have to identify the hatch.

If you are presenting to selective fish, you have to give the fish what is triggering it. Net the water and take a sample of the insects that are floating by. Then match the hatch.

If you aren't successful and you're not matching the hatch, keep moving until you find less selective fish.

If fish are rising but won't look at your offering, consider using midges. Often, trout take very small flies. If you can approximate the hatch—the most common midge pattern being a Griffiths gnat—you will catch fish. You'll need a long leader, a light tippet, and patience. Fish two flies at once. The first fly should be a large pattern that will serve as a sort of strike indicator. Tie the smaller second fly to the bend of the first hook. (This also works well with low-riding flies like spinners, emergers, and ants.)

Taking a selective fish is a challenge. You have to give the fish exactly what it's asking for.

Casting Where You Think the Fish Might Be

You're nearly always better off fishing to fish you can see working the top of the water. You can see where fish are, and you can home in on water known to produce fish. But fishing directly to the fish isn't always possible. So you go fish prospecting. You cover the water. You usually move upstream, an advantage since you approach the fish from their blind side. You will often be casting attractors and terrestrials.

Here's a nice brown Michael pulled from a swirl of conflicting currents.

Casting the Riffles

A lot of people are gun-shy about dry-fly casting. We've scared them a little with horror stories about drag, presentation, and perfect casting. Never mind that the horror stories are true. If you want to get your feet wet, literally and metaphorically, try casting to the riffles. It's a darn good place to start.

Riffles are also the easiest place to start, a water that is most forgiving.

Fishing the riffles means busting into the water and usually working upstream, casting to every likely spot as you go. The reason this is a great place to start is that *fish in the riffles are hungry.* They are in this water for no other reason than to feed.

This isn't pleasant water for a fish. Staying in the fast current burns up their valuable energy. Look for fish to be holding in water with structure that breaks up the current. Look for pools and eddies and places where a fish doesn't have to fight the current—but is still close enough to see what is drifting by. Look at the head and end of any small pools. Look around rocks and boulders.

The fish in riffles have little time to react, so they usually react quickly. They have to decide fast on taking a fly. If they don't, it's gone. In slow waters, you can almost feel the fish's pondering and hesitation before moving. Not in this water. There's a lot of food, but it's moving fast. It's to your advantage that the broken water makes it hard for the fish to see you.

How your fly floats is more important than a perfect selection of fly. We're dealing with a lot of currents, bubbles, and turbulence. You need a fly that stands out, a fly that can be seen by the fish. Flies that might perfectly match the hatch in a pool or flat will be useless in riffles if they can't be seen. You might want to increase the size of your fly. The Royal Wulff is considered to be one of the best flies for this type of fishing because it rides the currents well and is very visible. The Royal Coachman is another, as is the Humpy.

We proved the value of prospecting for fish in the riffles one summer day. The water was fairly low, the hatch was intense, and the big browns were going into feeding frenzies about 4:30 P.M. But as luck would have it, every one of our "secret" stretches of water was wall-to-wall with casters. So we plowed into the water and worked ¼ mile of riffle by the roadside. It's very accessible but rarely fished, perhaps because it's too obvious. We waded in shorts and tennis shoes.

Dave tied on his favorite Wulff pattern and headed over to the far side of the stream. Michael threaded on a Coachman and worked the side by the road. Dave told fishing lies about the ones that got away, while Michael recounted only slightly embellished stories about a trip he took to the Yukon. Michael slipped on a rock and got immersed. Dave stepped on a water snake. We worked our way up through the riffles, having a grand time. Within a couple of hours we'd both caught and released a number of fish, most of them small, but several of good size.

Movin' About

It's fun casting to a fish you see rising up to take a fly. But sometimes there's not a hatch on. Or there are bugs everywhere, but nothing seems to be breaking the surface. In this situation, movin' about with your fly rod in hand isn't all that unpleasant.

Michael tells about how he found his favorite water on Slough Creek in Yellowstone Park.

> I never had to wade more than 500 to 600 yards up the stream. I always seemed to catch the water during a hatch, so I fished the same holes again and again. This time I fished slowly, but without success for most of the day. I couldn't find a fish rising, so I started fishing and covering the water. I worked up several miles of stream. In addition to it being a wonderful journey, I discovered that I'd been overlooking some very incredible water. I was so stuck on fishing the hatch on the lower part of the stream, I never bothered to explore farther up. The water I stumbled onto was water that got a lot less fishing pressure, and it had bigger fish.

When you are fishing to rising fish, especially in deep water, you can stay in the same place for hours. But when you start fishing the water and not a specific fish, you are going to be moving.

The first thing you look for as you move about is good water: water that might hold fish.

You've studied chapter 4 and understand the concepts of reading water, so you'll spend most of your valuable fishing time casting to sections of stream that look promising. You'll especially be interested in casting to waters that might hold feeding or aggressive fish. Identify waters that are likely to be productive, waters where food is more available.

Cast to seams and to the mouths of little feeder streams. Don't overlook the foot of rapids, boulders, undercut banks, and other structure. You'll cover a lot of water in one day, making a cast or two at a likely spot, then moving. If you feel good about a stretch of water, work it a little more thoroughly. But for the most part, it's cast and move. If you find fish, or feeding fish, stop and fish them longer and more thoroughly.

Flies to Use

Which flies will you use? On some occasions you'll know which fly to use, and that's what you'll start with. Perhaps there's a specific hatch on, but the fish just aren't biting. It might be a good strategy to go with a proven pattern for that time of the year. There are many times, however, when you're just not sure what to tie on.

First, a general comment. Many casters' flies are too large! Start small, and tie on larger ones later, if necessary. As a rule, fish will more readily take a smaller pattern over a larger pattern. If fish are biting on a #16 fly, they'll take a #18 (which is smaller) but probably not a #14 (which is larger).

There may be something to the cliché that big flies take big fish. But sometimes, big flies take *no*

A Parachute Green Drake.

fish. When you're about to fish, and you don't know which fly to use, go small. Start out with #16–#18 patterns; perhaps even #20 in very low, clear water.

Flies designed to mimic specific insects are so localized that we'll cover only general attractors in this discussion. Attractors are a very good way to approach covering the water. The best attractors for this situation are the Adams, the Royal Coachman, the Royal Wulff, the Humpy, and the Irresistible, and the ant and hopper patterns.

Most agree that the Adams is the most commonly used and probably the best single fly for this type of fishing. But there will be days when it doesn't seem to work as well as the Coachman or the Wulff. With these three fly attractors, in various sizes, you'll be ready to fish. To add a little more power, throw in a few terrestrials. At times, if you can't match the size, the color, or the shape closely enough, the fish won't budge. But, if you throw something entirely different, like a terrestrial, you may tempt even the spookiest fish to come to the surface.

With these patterns, you can fish nearly any water successfully. Add a few local favorites, and nothing will stop you.

Types of Streams

We're not really sure where a creek becomes a stream and a stream becomes a river. We've all seen creeks and streams that ought to be called rivers and rivers that ought to be called streams. Where we live in the West, anything you can't jump across seems to be labeled a river.

Two types of streams merit a little extra attention because they are so often referred to in casting literature by name and because, in their extremes, they are fished differently.

Freestone Streams

One assumes that stream types get their name because they feature stones with lots of water running freely over them. These waters are tumbling, rapid, and quick dropping, filled with boulders and stones and heavily oxygenated. Small creeks and runoff usually provide the water for freestone streams, which can be either creeks or rivers.

This water, turbulent and moving, may not be clear, and the temperature might fluctuate a lot during the year. The fish in a freestone stream tend to be hungry. The water moves fast, so the fish are used to responding fast. This is to your advantage since the fish won't have long to look your fly over.

Start with a 4X or 5X leader and a #16 fly, a #16 ant, or a #10 hopper. If the water is very clear, or if it's in the dog days of summer when the water is low, you might want a fine tippet and a small fly. The best patterns are the Adams, the Royal Coachman, the Royal Wulff, the Blue Wing Olive, the ant, and the hopper.

Spring Creeks/Tailwaters

Spring creeks (sometimes called limestone creeks) get their water from an underground source. As a rule, the water is not moving as rapidly as a freestone stream, and the water temperature is much more stable and constant. The water is very clear.

With the number of dams on creeks and rivers these days, there is another word you should be familiar with—*tailwater*. A tailwater is the water that comes out of a dam. Because the water comes from the bottom of the dam, the temperature is steady (in the fifty to fifty-five degree range) year-round—creating spring creek-like conditions.

Fish in a true spring creek are hard to catch. The water is clear, so the fish can see you. There are often many nutrients in the water, giving fish a lot of food to select from. And the water is usually slow, allowing the fish time to make a selection. Everything about your presentation has to be correct or the fish will head back to the bottom of the stream. A drag-free float is essential.

Start with a 5X or 6X leader. Your dry flies should start at #18 (maybe even #20 if the fish spook easily or the water is low). Your ant should also be a #18, the hopper a #10. The best patterns are the Parachute Adams, the Blue Wing Olive, the Rusty Dun Spinner, the Trico Spinner, the ant, and the hopper. Depending on the size of the water, you may need to go a size larger or a size smaller. When in doubt, start small.

Some waters exhibit a combination of the characteristics of freestone streams and spring creeks. Waters coming from a dam or reservoir can be just like those of a spring creek. Utah's Green River is such an example. It looks like a freestone river but has many of the characteristics of a spring creek. Henry's Fork of the Snake River, in Idaho, is another.

13

FLOAT TUBES
AND OTHER STUFF

Getting to the Fish

Wading isn't always the best way to fish. Sometimes it's better to float.

There are a number of reasons why floating makes sense. Floating allows you to get to where the fish are, and it gives you a better angle on the fish because you can cast shoreward. It gives you a lot of freedom that shore standers don't have.

You can cast from anything that floats. For most of us, however, floating means a drift boat, a rubber raft, a small rowboat or powerboat, or a float tube.

It pays to be careful.

Last August Michael and his friend Kasey Cox were scouting a stretch of river via Coleman canoe. Michael was holding a casting seminar later in the week and wanted to put his casters on the best pools.

Negotiating a swift but shallow section of water before a trestle, the canoe hit a rock just below the surface. Someone zigged when he should have zagged. The canoe turned, and Kasey bailed out. While getting out, Michael got his leg caught under the canoe as it filled with water.

The weight of the water-filled canoe, sideways in the stream, flung Michael out while his leg was still pinned. The canoe finally floated off, but not before it slammed Mike's leg into a sharp rock,

A float tube in the the morning. A nice way to start a day!

scraping the bone and gouging deep into the muscle. Later we'd find out there was a green-stick break, too.

While the water wasn't deep, it was fast. Both were wearing excellent life jackets. Kasey, who was 50 yards downstream by this time, was able to catch our canoe, which weighed hundreds and hundreds of water-logged pounds.

Michael floated on his back until he could get his footing and scramble to shore. By this time, Michael was going into shock. He could hardly put weight on his leg, and it was bleeding like a stuck pig.

Kasey treated him for shock, dumped an entire bottle of antiseptic on the jagged cut, and loaded him in the canoe. By the time they got to the Bronco, Michael's lower leg was swollen double its normal size, and he couldn't put any weight on it.

Michael spent the next four weeks on his back, since his leg had gotten badly infected.

Accidents do happen, but doing things right softens the effects. Both were wearing life jackets and were able to get to shore easily. It's always a good idea to canoe in pairs in water that can be tricky. Kasey was able to help Mike after he went into shock. Could he have made it down the river by himself in shock? Maybe, but it's not something we'd recommend. A disoriented person working through tight turns in a canoe isn't a good thing. Kasey was able to take control and do the thinking.

We also had a first-aid kit in the boat. Did it help? It didn't hurt any.

This incident has reiterated the concept of boat and float-tube safety. Once you've punched your ticket, there is no more fly fishing. (Maybe that's not true—how can there be heaven without fly fishing?)

It's a family rule: As soon as Abbey gets her waders on, the next item is her life vest. She is not allowed in a float tube, kick boat, or canoe without a personal flotation device.

Being Safe and Happy

Being dead isn't happy, not for you or your family. On a less dramatic scale, taking an unexpected dip and losing a Sage rod and every fly you own isn't happy, either.

Dave wants you safe. Michael wants you happy. We want you to catch a lot of fish and become a great fly caster. So please remember the following points on safety when you float:

Always have life jackets for everyone. It's your life, so have a good-quality jacket. Cheap isn't better when you've capsized and are making your way to shore a mile away. (The Type III is safe and is very comfortable.)

Be informed about the water on which you are floating. Know when the winds come up and where the major boating lanes are. You're pretty helpless in a tube when a big ski boat bears down upon you. If you're in a canoe, the wakes from boats might present a problem.

Keep an eye on the weather. Watch for changes in the weather. It's better to come off the lake five dozen times when you don't need to than to be caught in the middle of a storm. *Lightning kills!* If the weather looks threatening, head close to shore so you can get off the water quickly. Live to fish another day.

Make yourself visible to boats. This is especially important with float tubes. Fluorescent colors on the back of the tube are easy to spot.

Use the buddy system. Go out with a buddy, especially if you are using a float tube. If there's trouble, the partner can help.

The Float Tube and You

For most of us, floating means a float tube: a belly boat, a donut, a tube, a kick boat, a float.

There's magic to a float tube. It puts you and your rod just inches above the water. It's just you and your tube, riding over the waves. You feel each swell; you feel the pulsing waves from passing skiers and bass boats. Being low on the water—half of you *in* the water—there's a certain enchantment to it. There are a lot of advantages, even though you are under kick power and can't cover the entire lake.

In the early days, a float tube was an inner tube with a nylon shell and a fabric seat. While the basic design is still the same, things have changed a lot. Most float tubes are still round, but some models no longer use the inner tube. Other models are U shaped so that getting in and out is easier.

Tubes are excellent for getting about shallow or snag-filled waters that are hard for boats to maneuver in. Tubes have a low profile in the water and don't seem to spook fish as much as a boat. Even in a heavy chop, belly boats are hard to flip over. And even folks with boats will often use tubes once they get to their fishing area.

Perhaps the greatest advantage is that they're easy to transport to the lake and easy to carry to the water. Once they are deflated, they're small enough to carry in a small knapsack. The advantages for the angler with a small car are obvious. But don't overlook carrying a belly boat into your favorite backcountry lake. Lakes that previously were fished only from the shore will take on a new dimension. When Dave and his friend, Ken, lugged belly boats into the mountains, they caught trout up to 20 inches long in lakes that formerly gave up only pan-size fish. They were able to float out to a rock island that had been off-limits before. Although the float tube and fins added a little weight to the hike, they discovered it was well worth the effort. They lashed the deflated tubes to the outside of the packs and hustled up the mountain. A passing packer, who had had little luck during his trip, thought the tubes were so handy that he offered to buy one of the outfits for double the price originally paid or rent one for $25 an hour.

Lakes or ponds in your area that aren't accessible by road could offer excellent fishing. High country lakes are paradise. On an annual canoe trip to Idaho, we packed along float tubes. We set up a base camp, hiked into high lakes, and fished the day away for the elusive golden trout. The float tubes were so successful that we took them on a canoe trip to Yellowstone.

Selecting a Tube

A float tube isn't expensive. For the price of the smallest trolling motor, you can purchase three or four nice float tubes. A moderately priced tube will serve you for years.

Make sure the fabric is heavy, the seams are double or triple stitched, and the zippers are of the highest quality. Also make sure there is a second tube that will act as a safety bladder. Every now and then, a tube will fail. Usually you'll know you're losing air and will have time to get to shore—but why take a chance? *Never buy a tube without a secondary safety bladder.*

Small men, women, and younger casters don't need a tube as large as one needed by a 200-pound man. A tube too small is a safety hazard, and you'll get your arms and elbows wet and be uncomfortable. A larger tube will allow you to ride higher in the water. Get a tube that is the right size for you; when in doubt, go larger. If you weigh 175 pounds or more, get the largest tube.

Make sure your tube has a back rest. Also look for a buckle on the seat. The buckle makes the tube easier to get in and out. If you should take a tumble, you can undo the seat strap and slide out easily. Get a tube with large pockets. Also look for a tube with D-rings to hang stuff on.

Many tubes have a blaze orange backing so it can be seen by zooming skiers, Jet Skiers, and boaters. If your tube doesn't have this orange, buy a yard of blaze orange fabric at a fabric store and secure it to your tube. Some tubers use a blaze flag.

Use your tube only in calm water. Floating all but the calmest rivers is risky and should be avoided. When you first start floating, keep close to shore. You'll be using some muscles; remember, you're under kick power. Until you learn how to judge the water, don't go out very far.

One day while we were fishing for cutthroat trout at a large reservoir, a wind came up. Dave was out in the channel and knew he could not kick his way back to shore, so he let the wind take his tube the dozen or so miles to the dam. When he got there, Michael was waiting. We have a standing agreement to meet at the dam in just such an event. Michael saw Dave sail off and knew where to go and get him.

When the wind comes up and you are in a channel, there's often not a lot you can do to fight it. On small lakes and ponds this might not be a problem. But what if you're out in the channel of Yellowstone Lake and the wind takes you south, away from the roads and into the wilderness?

Find out when the wind normally comes up and which ways it blows. Winds on lakes are fairly predictable. Stay close enough to shore so you can get back. You can fight the wind for a while, but your legs will probably give out before the zephyr does.

When you are fishing from a float tube, have a point of land or a nearby shore that you can head to. Tube in inlets and bays. If you want to go off points into main channels, do so cautiously.

You and the Canoe

Dave is the undisputed expert in canoeing and has taught Michael the finer points. Dave and his wife spent the first summer they were married around Jackson Hole, Wyoming, where he was a river/fishing guide. Dave lived out of a canoe and did a lot of fishing from it.

Not long after Michael got his first canoe, a red Coleman, Dave dropped by Mike's house to show off a new rod he'd just built. Michael's wife, Shari, didn't say a word as she pointed to the irrigation ditch in the back field. Dave walked around the

A canoe can be a perfect way to fish a mountain lake.

house and through a field, new rod in hand. And there was Michael, standing in the Coleman in the middle of the water, barely drifting with the current, casting tight loops toward the grassy edges of the steep cutaway bank.

A guy in a canoe in the middle of a cornfield? This isn't something you'd expect to see. But, when Michael set the hook on a 15-inch German brown, Dave ran back to his Jeep and grabbed his fishing vest.

"It's great," Michael shouted as he paddled the canoe to the bank so Dave could hop in. "There's a lot of high water, and fish from the river get sucked up into the canal. They hang around this bend—lots of food and shelter. I fish it from the bank every summer, but this is the best I've seen it. I think it's the canoe."

When Dave's wife called at 9:00 that evening, the boys were still at it. The neighbors shook their heads and went back to barbecuing. Dave's wife fed his dinner to the dog.

It's Fun, but Be Careful

A canoe, like a float tube, is an effective way to expand your fishing waters. You don't have to have a trailer, you don't have to mortgage the family home, the canoe is easy to store, and it can provide great fun for the family when you're not fishing out of it. A canoe can be carried by one person, and it can fit on your car.

A canoe has limitations. Take it one step at a time. A canoe is a wonderful tool, but it's not safe to take in choppy water. In the chop, you're far safer in the float tube, which will ride the waves. A canoe is quicker and more mobile. But on many lakes, the afternoon water is just too choppy for canoeing. Canoes are wonderful in the morning and evening.

When there's a mist on the water, and the sun is just coming up, there's nothing more beguiling than casting from your canoe. Don't get too beguiled and

Fishing from a canoe on calm water like this is very rewarding, but head for shore if conditions turn choppy.

A canoe like this one is a good fishing companion.

forget to wear your flotation device, however. Spending years as a guide out of Jackson, Wyoming, Dave's observation is worth paying attention to:

> Most of the times that I've seen or heard about a canoe tipping, it wasn't in white water or in choppy, windy conditions from a storm that just blew in, catching the paddlers by surprise. Nearly always it was in gentle water where the boaters thought they were safe and under control.

There are a number of good books on the subject. The best one we can think of is *The Complete Book of Canoeing* by I. Herbert Gordon (The Globe Pequot Press). If you enjoy waterskiing or bass tourneys, a huge engine is necessary. The rev of a powerful engine and the scream of raw power as pistons pound isn't a bad thing. There comes a time, however, when it's nice to leave the noise and fumes behind and get more in tune with the water. Maybe you simply want to escape to a quiet, gentle way. There's something relaxing about canoeing. There's something even more serene about casting from a canoe. It takes you back to quieter times, to a calm tradition of fishing in the days of yore.

Aesthetics aside, it's a super way to fish compared with a float tube. You can cover more water, and since you are sitting above the water, you can get more distance with your cast. Sitting up is especially handy when fishing for patrolling bass because the fish are easier to spot and thus easier to fish. A canoe also is warmer. No matter how well dressed you are, sooner or later the water starts to get to you when you're tubing. In a canoe, there's room to keep your stuff. You can spread out your fly boxes. The worst that can happen is that they fall to the bottom of the craft. This is preferred to having them float away from your float tube when your back is turned.

Some folding boats, like this Porte-Boat, transport easily to the water.

Other Things That Float

Anything that you can float and cast from is suitable, whether paddle-powered or motor-powered.

A good rowboat can be a godsend, but it's tough lugging a rowboat about. There are other options, including folding boats and rubber rafts. Both offer first-rate assists for the fly caster. A folding boat or rubber raft can be carried by one person and can be transported in the family car (or on top of the car).

When you look for a rubber raft, check the number of air chambers and the weight of the material. A cheap model can serve you well, but it won't last as long, and it might be harder to paddle than a better version. You have to be careful that you don't tear the sides.

I've used a friend's folding boat on a number of waters. It's our official striper boat on Lake Powell. With a small motor, it bobs over the waves and has provided many happy fishing hours.

A folding boat will fit on top of your car. You don't have to mess with trailers or other traditional hassles.

Floating Fishing Methods

Whether you are fishing from a boat, a canoe, or a float tube, the method of fishing is still the same. It's you, the fly, and the water.

A kick boat.

During the summer, we often keep canoes strapped to the top of our rigs so we can take off at a moment's notice. An inexpensive canoe has served us well.

This fish became our dinner after Dave caught him in his kick boat.

Basic Wet-Fly Fishing on Lakes and Ponds

Depending on how deep the fish are, you'll want a sink line, a sink tip line, or a floating line with a long leader. (With a sink line you can fish down to 20 feet; with a sink tip you can fish from 4 to 7 feet [helpful when you are fishing over a moss bed]; a floating line with a shot is good from 3 to 5 feet.)

With a sinking line, you'll use a short leader; there's no need for a taper. (Often you'll be fishing a 2X to 4X line from 3 to 5 feet in length.)

Retrieving the Fly

The first thing to remember is to *count*. If you simply cast your fly and let it drop and catch a fish, you won't have any idea how deep the fish are. To keep things straight, count as your fly sinks. This way you can fish systematically and cover the water consistently. You'll know you are varying the depths that your pattern reaches by letting it drop for varying amounts of time (counts).

Remember, on a lake you give your fly all its action. With the line under your index finger of the hand holding the rod, use the hand that holds your line to make stripping retrieves. *Vary the action and the manner of retrieve.*

Strip in some line, and then pause. Vary the retrieve and the lengths of line coming in—as well as how long you pause so the pattern just sits or sinks—until you find what action the fish want. Essentially, what you are doing is jigging your fly. If you've jigged with a spinning rod, this will be very similar. You're jigging your pattern.

There is no set way that will work all the time. If the fish are aggressive or hungry, they'll take anything you throw at them. If they are more neutral, you're going to have to work for them and give them the pattern of fly movement they seem to want. The beauty of jigging is that you have to constantly adjust your technique to match the fish's mood.

Use a rapid retrieve with aggressive fish and a slow speed with more neutral fish.

One of our favorite ways to retrieve the fly consists of the following sequence: a series of short little jerks followed by a long pause; more short jerks, then a long pause; a few short jerks, then a *short* pause; a couple of *long* jerks, then a long pause. Then repeat.

While there are many ways you can work your line, there are some standard retrieves. A useful one is the *steady retrieve*. Here you wrap incoming line around your hand, ensuring a steady movement. With your line hand, grab the fly line between your thumb and index finger and bring it toward your body. Your pinky should be pointing toward the tip of the rod. Turn your wrist over so line wraps around your pinky and pulls toward you. Grab incoming line with thumb and index finger and twist over your hand. Move to the original position and start again. With a little practice this becomes a smooth process, and you'll get a steady retrieve.

To get a more erratic, wounded-fish retrieve, use mixed short and long pulls on the line. Make sure to pause.

To set the hook, *pull down sharply with your line hand* rather than lifting the rod. This will set the hook very nicely. Then simply lift the rod. If you miss your fish, your fly will still be in the strike zone.

Favorite Flies

Soon you'll have your own preferred lake flies. Until you do, let us suggest some favorite wets. These flies account for more than 90 percent of the fish we've taken on lakes and ponds:

- Wooly Bugger (all colors) #4 to #10
- Damsel Nymph #6 to #10
- Marabou Leech #1/0 to 12
- Bucktail #1/0 to 10
- Marabou Muddler #1/0 to 10
- Scud #10 to #16

Sometimes the only way you can work salmon water effectively is from a boat. These fine fish are on their way to be smoked.

Basic Dry-Fly Fishing on Lakes and Ponds

The first thing to do is match the hatch just as you would in rivers and streams. Take your bug screen and run it through the water for 10 or 20 feet. Look at the samples you have collected and try to duplicate them.

Matching the Hatch

Lake and pond trout are sometimes more selective in what they eat. There is no conveyer-belt current bringing food to their lie. Instead, these fish move to the food. They can afford to be choosy and study what they eat. Your presentation has to be just right.

If you don't have any luck, try different sizes of the same pattern. Sometimes a change in size will trigger a response. In a stream, the rule when you're not having any luck is to go smaller. On a lake, try both larger and smaller. And if you have to choose, go larger. It seems that a bigger bite will sometimes trigger a response.

Attractor Patterns

If you can't match the hatch, or matching the hatch doesn't work, try attractors. Attractors work very well, perhaps even better on a lake than on rivers and streams.

We know several fishermen, not yet converted to the glorious fly rod, who have fished in many of the finest backwaters on this continent. Other than a few spinners, their tackle consists of a half dozen attractor patterns in various sizes, a few clear floats, and some shot to make the flies wet. These anglers have caught a lot of nice fish and have the pictures to prove it. While we regret the satisfaction and enjoyment they have lost by using a less than satisfactory fishing outfit, no one can argue with how successful a few good attractor patterns are.

Working the Fish

Watch the water carefully and look for signs of feeding fish. It is always better to cast to a fish that is feeding than to just cast randomly. It takes a little bit of practice to locate fish, but it's not that hard. Casters call this "working the fish." With a pair of good glasses and a brimmed hat, you'll be set. This is harder to do from a float tube since you don't have as high a vantage point as someone sitting in a boat.

Once you locate surface rings of a fish feeding or actually see the fish patrolling the water, watch to see if you can locate a feeding pattern.

If you notice rings or bubbles on the surface, pay attention to the pattern. Draw an imaginary ring around the area. With your first cast, you'll want your fly and leader on the imaginary perimeter, but not your fly line. Work the edges, casting progressively farther and farther into the imaginary ring. Work the water thoroughly.

If you have spotted fish, don't cast directly to them (unless they happen to be very aggressive and seem to be taking everything). Try to determine where you think the fish are going next. (Some lake and pond trout have patterns that are predictable.) Place your fly in front of the fish's path. If you get your fly on the film before the fish is in the area, you won't spook it with your line.

What do you do when there's not a thing in sight, or just an occasional ring here and there? At times like this, you might want to try fishing wet. But wet or dry, you need to decide on a good area. Review the chapter on wet-fly and dry-fly fishing and the chapter on reading the water (chapter 4). Make sure you're fishing in waters that fish are in. Be aware of water temperatures, and look for where a fish might find food and shelter. Always fish structure first. Some of our favorites are moss lines, confluences of streams, and off points of land.

A nice grayling Michael caught in a kick boat next to shore. This fish took a leach pattern Michael was stripping in very slowly.

Favorite Flies

You'll want to add your own favorites. But in the meanwhile, let us suggest some of our favorites:

- Double Ugly #12 to #16
- Griffiths Gnat #18 to #20
- Damsel Fly #6 to #10
- Gray Hackle Yellow #12 to #8
- Black Gnat #16 to #18
- Mosquito #14 to #18
- Royal Wulff #14 to #18
- Royal Coachman #14 to #20

Both Wet and Dry

Sometimes you'll want the best of both worlds, so you'll go both wet and dry. This is a good way to fly fish when you're trying to determine whether wet or dry will be the most effective. It involves fishing with both a wet fly and a dry fly at the same time. This technique is an excellent way to fish clear, high-mountain lakes and beaver dams.

If you catch a few fish in a row on the wet fly, you'll be tempted to go wet, but don't. Stay with both, because the dry fly makes a good strike indicator for the wet fly. If all the fish are hooked on the dry fly, go dry. If you're getting them both ways, stay as you are. This is one of our favorite techniques for fishing in lakes where feeding or patrolling fish are visible.

Here's how the wet-and-dry technique works: Tie a dry fly onto the leader. If you haven't identified a hatch, tie on an attractor pattern (perhaps a Royal Wulff, an Adams, an Elk Hair Caddis, a Royal Coachman, a Double Ugly, a Damsel, or a Gray Hackle Yellow). Select a fly that rides well in the water. From the shank of the hook, tie a 2- to 3-foot section of tippet. On this section of line, tie on a small fly (a midge pupa or something similar, like the Serendipity). Above this fly attach a micro shot to get it down into the water.

(Some anglers don't like to run a tippet off the dry fly. Instead they prefer working with a really long tippet. On the end of the tippet, they attach the wet fly. They go up a few feet and attach a stiff leader. From this *dropper* they attach the dry fly. The stiff leader helps keep the flies and leaders from getting twisted. When the fly is tied on, the stiff leader should be no more than 2 to 4 inches long.)

Be sure to give the dry fly a good dose of floatant so that it floats visibly. You'll want to watch the dry fly; it will be your makeshift strike indicator. If it bobs, set the hook. It means a fish is going for the wet fly. If a fish goes for the dry fly, you'll see the disruption on the surface. Set the hook.

These are some excellent proven combinations you might consider:

- Double Ugly with Serendipity
- Royal Wulff with Pheasant Tail Nymph
- Damsel with Brassie

Mix and match. Almost any combination will work.

The Double:
Excellent for Mountain Lakes
and Beaver Ponds

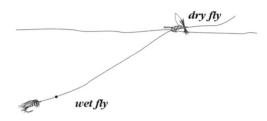

Flies to Use
Dry fly:	*Wet fly:*
• *Coachman*	• *Pheasant tail*
• *Royal Wulff*	• *Brassie*
• *Double Ugly*	• *Hare's Ear*

For beaver ponds and mountain lakes, fish a dry fly (something very visible) with a wet-fly chaser (with a micro shot). Watch the dry fly—it's a strike indicator of sorts. You can fish the best of both worlds.

CASTING OUT AND ABOUT

Walking with a Fly Rod

Leave the cell phone at home. Leave the appointment calendar, too. Better yet, drop them both in the nearest trash can. Leave the PDA in the fridge, and shove the laptop into the closet. Ready to break away from the throng with only your favorite rod and a handful of trusty flies? It's easy. Just strap on your walking shoes and get off the beaten path. As a fly caster, you'll love the wilderness you can see only on foot. Walking also helps expand the potential of your local waters and improves your fishing averages.

Expanding Local Waters: Beating the Crowds

"Beating the crowds" does not only mean heading off to the Tetons or the New Hampshire mountain country. Yes, it can mean backcountry fishing. But we're also talking about something as simple as putting distance between you and the parking lot, between you and the crowds.

You can go on only so many major blue-ribbon fishing trips a year. In the meanwhile, you still want to fish, so you'll naturally hit the waters close by, places you can easily drive to. You may not have

Getting away from the crowds not only means solitude, it means better fishing. Throwing your waders, rod, and vest into a day pack and hiking down a trail can yield excellent results. Dave has found just such a place—but he won't tell us where it is.

Beating the Crowd

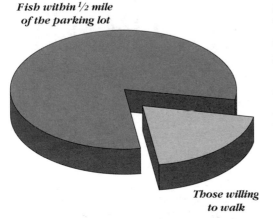

Fish within ½ mile of the parking lot

Those willing to walk

Carrying in a tube to lakes and ponds is a good way to take advantage of the backcountry.

enough time or money to travel too far, but you've got to fish.

Local fishing is not a bad idea. Often fishing is good near your back door. And even if it isn't, oh well—any fishing is better than no fishing. But occasionally there's a problem: too many people on your favorite water.

If you've ever tried to fish in water that a dozen other anglers have worked through in the past few hours, you'll know that the fishing can be more than tough. The fish are spooked, and since there's a lot of fishing pressure, they've seen about every presentation. The fish that survive become ultraselective. Have you ever parked your car and rushed to your favorite pool only to find several other anglers casting from your best spot?

The problem is worse when the weather is good and on weekends. In the off-season and when it's cold or raining, you will probably have the water to yourself. Although crowds can be frustrating, don't despair. You can beat the crowd.

Park and Walk

If you're willing to walk a little, you can eliminate a lot of the problem. Why? *Because most fishermen and -women never get more than ½ mile from where they parked the car!* If you are willing to burn a little shoe leather, you'll be in better fishing water in fifteen minutes. If you are willing to hike a half hour to an hour, you'll dramatically separate yourself from the crowds.

Most people don't want to work any harder than they have to. People who fish are no different. But if you're willing to burn a few extra calories, you can get into the best fishing. You may have to cross a few fields, stare down a milk cow or two, walk over a hill, and fight a little brush. But it will be worth it. The most frustrating thing is walking past water without stopping to fish it.

On the Green River, a major part of the fishing pressure is close to several parking areas. If a caster hikes a mile or so before starting to fish, the crowds thin out dramatically. The same is true in our national parks, some of which, at times during the summer, can feel like crowded subways. If you walk half a mile or so from where people park, you'll notice very few people.

When you're fishing, you can cover a mile or two and not notice it. But try walking that far in neoprene chest waders, and you'll feel it, especially if it's a warm day. Better yet, hike in a pair of running shoes and carry your waders and boots (or put them in a day pack).

Running shoes are light. They can be stuffed in your pack or vest while you fish. Or you can hide them behind a rock, ready to put back on when you're set to hike out. Nothing is more miserable than trying to hike in hot, nonbreathing waders.

Backcountry Fishing

Backcountry fishing involves getting into country that can be seen only through hiking, country that can be rugged and wild. If you don't like to backpack, you can still get into the backcountry in a long day hike.

Either way—day hike or overnight—there are a couple of things you have to consider. The first is that the fishing is usually pretty good, so you'll have a great time. The other is that this country can be difficult and unforgiving; you have to enter it prepared.

In some areas—like sections of the Sierras, the Wind River Range, the Bob Marshall Wilderness, the Pacific Crest Trail—the road to the trailhead may still be covered with snow in early June. Ice still covers mountain lakes. During the short summer, fish go on a two-month feeding frenzy. They have to pack away a lot of energy for the long, cold months to come.

This spells good fishing for you, because the fish will take whatever looks good. There are some

Camping in the mountains is a great way to get away from the crowds.

A hike away from the beaten path will get you to water that hasn't been heavily fished.

Before you head off to fish the wilds, shake down your gear to make sure it's all there and in working order.

All you need for an adventure away from the madding crowd is a fly rod, a day pack, and some imagination.

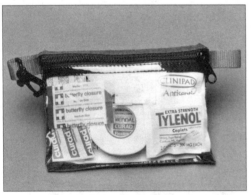

It's a good idea to have a small first-aid kit in your pack to take care of unplanned emergencies.

glorious hatches on the water, and it's a wonderful time to be a fly caster. But if the fishing shuts down on a lake, no problem; just move to another lake nearby.

A successful backcountry caster is one who moves from water to water.

The beauty of backcountry fishing is that each water is different. Rarely will all the lakes in a drainage be all hot or all cold for fishing. Fish on one lake will be finicky, but fish on another only a quarter mile away are waiting to jump into your net. A Sierras guide told Michael: "I move my people about until we hit the hottest water, and that's where we stay."

Lakes will usually have the biggest fish in the backcountry, but streams and beaver dams also will provide hours of fishing excitement.

Fishing Tips

This book has covered the techniques that will make you a successful fly caster, and these same techniques will work for you in the backcountry. You've learned about reading the water, and you understand something about the fish's needs. You've learned some wet and dry-fishing strategies. You also have an idea about what flies to carry.

If we might belabor the obvious, on mountain lakes, look for structure: fallen logs, boulders, points, and confluences. These will be excellent places to look for fish. Don't forget to fish the wet-and-dry combinations we described at the end of chapter 13. It's an excellent way to take trout.

Take a supply of patterns in various sizes, and check the area to see if some local favorites need to be added to your box. Stock up on attractors. And don't forget terrestrials in several sizes. (Hint: An ant is most deadly on a high mountain lake.)

Footwear

In some cases, running shoes can make excellent hiking shoes. There is a lot of cushion and support, and they are light. (Remember that every pound of footwear is equivalent to six to ten pounds on your back.)

Sometimes running shoes aren't quite enough. Perhaps the trail is muddy or steep, there are a lot of rocks, you're carrying a heavy pack, or you have weak ankles.

It's then a good idea to wear something heavier. There has been a revolution in hiking and backpacking boots. They have lightened up considerably, they can be waterproof and breathable, they offer better support—and the boots are more comfortable.

The old style of hiking boot has gone the way of the dinosaur and the Edsel. High-tech boots are now more like running shoes and less like technical mountaineering boots. For many modern boots, there isn't even a break-in period.

Michael writes articles on backpacking and hiking and has logged many miles on backcountry trails, from northern Alaska to the Yukon, from the Olympic Peninsula to Mexico. This is his report:

A good pair of running shoes is a great way to get to your fishing area. Shoes also work when you are sorting out a snarled fly box.

When I hike, I wear a New Balance running shoe, the 841 or 972, because these shoes are light, but sturdy and trailworthy—and they fit my feet well. If I'm in rougher terrain or the weather is colder, I'll wear a good walking boot. For me, a good boot must be light, but made from a sturdy leather, a boot with a great deal of support. (I also want a Gore-Tex liner so it's waterproof.) I've tried literally every boot on the market when I've done comparison articles. For me, Vasque makes the best boot for the money— a boot that is light, sturdy, lasts a long time—and I don't have to take out a bank loan to purchase it. I want a boot that will give me years of wear. If I'm hiking in very wet, really boggy terrain, I might wear a rubber pac (L.L. Bean or Cabella's makes good models). These are not overly expensive pieces of footwear and they are very easy to find. Often on a packing trip I'll take both: running shoes and a pair of boots. My running shoes are so light they'll tuck in any odd place. This way I have the best of both worlds.

A can of pepper spray is a must if you are fishing in bear country.

Wear boots that fit. In a mostly leather boot, you can expect a certain amount of stretch. In a boot with synthetic fabric, there will be little or no stretching; don't buy the boot and expect to fit into it as you wear it.

Remember to take to the shoe store the socks you are going to wear in the field. It will do you little good to buy a hiking boot with the wrong socks on. Besides getting a pair of boots that fit, wear the right socks. For most people, this means two pair: a lightweight polypropylene or nylon sock topped by a heavier wool or ragg sock.

Blisters can usually be avoided. Prevent blisters by protecting sensitive areas, especially heels, with moleskin. But when you get a blister, take care of it immediately. Drain it and cover the area with moleskin. Moleskin should be in every hiker's kit.

What to Take

What should you take along into the backcountry?

If you're fishing near home, less than a mile from the car, all you need is your casting gear. But if you are going farther back—and it's easy to cover from 8 to 12 miles a day—you'll be a long way from the trailhead, your vehicle, or others. You'll have to make do with what you pack with you.

Many times Dave will leave at dawn and come back after dark. It makes for a long, exhausting day, but it's a lively way to see the backcountry and get into the good fish. But whether you are gone for just one long day or for ten days, there are several things you'll need to carry. The high country is fickle, and a weather forecast for the valley may have little bearing. In many areas, it rains every afternoon. No hiker or packer should leave the trailhead or take off crosscountry without rain gear. Whether you favor a poncho or a rain suit, lightweight models are available and should be standard gear for any packer.

There is nothing like a wilderness fly-fishing camp.

Other common-sense items you ought to have are a knife, matches, fire starter, compass, map of the area, light jacket, first-aid kit, small survival kit, food, and water.

Don't count on drinking the local waters. Unless the water is coming right from the ground, we can't think of a region that is free from contamination such as *giardia*. You may opt to pack a canteen or carry one of the excellent water filters on the market these days.

Everyone has an opinion on the best trail food. Just be sure to carry enough of whatever you like to eat. And carry a little extra in case you get stuck. Several of the new high-energy bars are excellent.

Before you leave, tell someone where you are going in case something goes wrong. Keep an eye on the weather, catch lots of fish, and have fun.

INDEX

About the Authors

For Michael Rutter, fishing is a way of life. His motto is fish first, and life will take care of itself. He has thrown flies throughout North America, from the Rocky Mountains and Alaska to the West Coast and the South. He has written hundreds of fishing articles for general outdoors magazines including *Outdoor Life* and *Sports Afield* as well as specialized fly fishing articles for *Fly Fishing* and *The Fly-fisher*. He has written forty books, including *Camping Made Easy* and *Fun with the Family in Utah*. Michael teaches technical and creative writing at Brigham Young University and lives with his family in Orem, Utah.

Dave Card is a well-known fishing instructor and writer who has written fishing articles for *Utah Fishing* and *Outdoors* magazine. Dave is a fishing guide and leads trips throughout the West. His clients have included rocker Ted Nugent and baseball player Kelly Downs. He teaches fly fishing and fly-tying classes and lectures at many fishing seminars and shows. Dave makes his home in Alpine, Utah.